D0092234

# The Battle of the Ages

Lance Lambert

Copyright © 2014
Lance Lambert

Two-fish Publications
Corona, California
Two-Fish Publications @ gmail.com
All Rights Reserved


Available at:

*www.createspace.com/4737978
(include numbers)
*www.amazon.com (Also Amazon worldwide)
*www.barnesandnoble.com


ISBN-13: 978-1497493537
ISBN-10: 1497493536

# CONTENTS

\* Preface ........................................5

1 Let us Watch and be Sober ..........................7

2 This World is Essentially Spiritual ...........................23

3 The Word of God and theTestimony of Jesus ...........41

4 The Strategic Necessity of Intercession ...................55

5 I Sought for a Man to Stand in the Gap.....................71

6 The Two-Fold Promise of God to Abraham..............93

7 He Will Set up an Ensign for The Nations ...............111

\* Epilogue: The Mystery of Israel ...............................127

# PREFACE

This book is a call and a challenge to genuine intercession and is directed to the remnant of the faithful in the Western nations, once called Christian nations. Those nations are witnessing a growing rapid paganization which will lead to great loss and to demonism. At the same time, there is a violent assault on the existence and being of the Living God and on the trustworthiness of His Word. The result is a growing apostasy. We desperately need a new breath of God renewing and reviving genuine believers and creating a living and working faith in Him. Nothing less than a spiritual awakening of huge proportion, in which multitudes would come to the Lord and experience His salvation, can change the direction of those nations which were once called the homeland of Christian missions.

I have entitled this book: "The Battle of the Ages". That battle has never ceased from the beginning of time as we know it. It is clear to me that the climax of the battle is ahead of us, and we need to know what we face and the safety we have in the Lord Jesus. In Him, we have absolute protection. He is our armor for the conflict, and we need to know how to stand, withstand, and having done all continue to stand in Him and in His power and strength. If once we learn to abide in the Lord Jesus, to remain where God has placed us, by the Holy Spirit we will overcome.

This book has grown out of a number of messages I gave to young people and to an IFA conference (Intercessors for America) which was held at the Inn of the Last Resort near Franklin, North Carolina. From the transcripts of the messages which I gave, this book has grown to seven chapters and an epilogue. It has been written in the midst of much difficulty of one kind or another and ongoing spiritual conflict, which considering the title is not surprising!

I wish to thank Craig and Inja Lewis of California for reducing the original messages into transcript form and urging me to turn them into a book. I also wish to thank Helen Reiss of Jerusalem for proofreading the chapters and for her invaluable help and fellowship in the work. I also want to thank Michael Hungerford of North Carolina for reducing the expansion into typed form and making many suggestions helpful and otherwise. May the Lord greatly bless this book and give His light and revelation to all who read it, and may it result in those who answer the call and challenge to genuine intercession in the situation that we face.

Lance Lambert
Jerusalem, May 2014

# Chapter One

## LET US WATCH AND BE SOBER

But concerning the times and the seasons, brethren, ye have no need that aught be written unto you. For yourselves know perfectly that the day of the Lord so cometh as a thief in the night. When they are saying, Peace and safety, then sudden destruction cometh upon them, as travail upon a woman with child; and they shall in no wise escape. But ye, brethren, are not in darkness, that that day should overtake you as a thief for ye are all sons of light, and sons of the day: we are not of the night, nor of darkness; so then let us not sleep, as do the rest, but let us watch and be sober. (1 Thessalonians 5:1-6)

If the foundations be destroyed, what can the righteous do? (Psalms 11:3)

Finally, be strong in the Lord, and in the strength of his might. Put on the whole armor of God that ye may be able to stand against the wiles of the devil. For our wrestling is not against flesh and blood, but against the principalities, against the powers, against the world-rulers of this darkness, against the spiritual hosts of wickedness in the heavenly places. Wherefore take up the whole armor of God that ye may be able to withstand in the evil day, and having done all, to stand. Stand therefore. (Ephesians 6:10-14a)

### WAKE UP

In this passage from the first Thessalonian letter which the apostle Paul wrote, he is warning us not to sleep as the world is asleep and indeed as are also many Christians, but to: "Wake up." It is a wakeup call! The fact of the matter is that although we have the Bible and God's Prophetic Word, very much of the Church is asleep. We are coasting along complacently and as the Lord said to the Laodicean Church; He is not in the midst but outside knocking on the door and saying: *Behold, I stand at the door and knock: if any man hear my voice and open the door, I will come in to him, and will sup with him and he with me (Revelation 3:20).* Could you believe that the Lord Jesus could say of any Church or Assembly: "I am outside, not on the inside. I am actually outside and knocking on the door. If anyone—not all of you—but if anyone single person can hear My voice and open the door I will come in and will sup with him and he with me."

The Apostle wrote of being spiritually asleep. What he wrote was and still is a serious warning for the last days:

> But ye, brethren, are not in darkness, that that day should overtake you as a thief for ye are all sons of light, and sons of the day: we are not of the night, nor of darkness; so then let us not sleep, as do the rest, but let us watch and be sober. (See 1 Thessalonians 5:4-6)

The word *watch* in English is the Greek word *gregoreo* which means to be awake, alert, or vigilant. The word *sober* in English is the Greek word *nepho* which simply means to be free from the influence of intoxicants. If we are not awake, alert, vigilant, and free from the intoxicating power of our self-life and the world, we shall be swept away. It will be an avalanche of evil, a flood of enormous proportions which will sweep us away, as it will sweep away the world! Those are very serious words for us all, but especially for young people who have had a Christian background and who think they know it all; to them "it is all old hat." They know how to say the right words and use the right phraseology because they have heard it all their lives. However, they may not be awake and there are many worldly influences which intoxicate us. For all of us, it is possible to be intoxicated and asleep, and not realize that what we have heard for years *will* finally happen in the end and maybe in our day.

Let us Watch and be Sober

Many of us may be rightly awaiting the rapture, but the fact remains that we may have some time through which to pass before that event takes place. The apostle Paul in his second letter to the Thessalonians wrote that we shall not be caught up to be with the Lord until the man of sin is revealed (see 2 Thessalonians 2:3b). That clearly implies that we will pass into the first period of deep spiritual darkness and trouble before the rapture takes place. If we, especially the younger ones, do not wake up now and begin to allow the Holy Spirit to prepare us, we will be taken by surprise.

## STORMS EXPOSE THE INWARD LIFE

One time when I was staying in Bowling Green, Virginia, there was a violent storm which knocked out the whole power in the area for many hours. When we awoke the next morning and went out in the area, I noticed that a large number of huge trees had been destroyed, but they were all rotten inside. Outwardly they looked marvelous, full of leaves, but when the trees were broken and downed we could tell that they had rotted from within. I thought to myself, "What a *warning* that is for all of us. Outwardly we may look fine and spiritual—with green leaves, singing the hymns, taking part in prayer—but when the storm comes, it exposes a hidden rot and lifelessness, or worse still hidden sin."

I remember a story which Charles Haddon Spurgeon recorded. He used to stay in a little fishing town in Devon for his holidays, in the Southwest of Britain. He loved it very much and he would go for a walk every evening as the sun was setting. It was the same fishing town where the hymn, "Abide with me, fast falls the even tide" was written. He would look at all the fishing boats and other kinds of boats which looked so beautiful in the harbor. Then came a dramatic and powerful storm. The following day, after it had passed, he went for his walk again. He noticed that at least

9

half of the boats had disappeared and he asked one of the nearby fishermen, "Why have so many of the boats sunk?" The old fisherman replied, "The boats that sank had too many barnacles." Those barnacles were not apparent because they were under the water line, but when the storm came those boats sank. Spurgeon said, "That is the kind of warning that only the Lord can give to us." Barnacles are those little crusty-looking creatures that grow on the boat under the water and actually make it heavy so that when the storm comes the boat sinks. It is a warning. Most of us have besetting sins which are not apparent to others, but when the storms of life hit us, it becomes apparent.

## WITNESSING A TOTAL COLLAPSE

The statement in Hebrew in Psalm 11:3 is very interesting. Both the King James Version and my version, which is the American Standard Version of 1901, which I consider to be one of the most accurate versions, reads like this: *If the foundations be destroyed, what can the righteous do?* However my version has an alternative marginal reading: *If the foundations be destroyed; what hath the righteous wrought?* The Hebrew here is very interesting, and has given rise to differing translations in various versions. For instance, Young's Literal Translation renders it like this: *If the foundations be destroyed, what have the righteous done?* That is also what my margin says: *What hath the righteous wrought?* The Jewish Publication Society's Bible renders it in the same way as the American Standard Version's marginal alternative. The Geneva Bible of 1587 also translates it: *What hath the righteous done?* Both Brenton's and Bagster's Septuagint in English render it: *What has the righteous done?* The Hebrew simply rendered is: "When the foundations have been destroyed, what have the righteous

10

done?" It shifts the responsibility for the collapse and disorder on the inactivity of the righteous. In other words, the righteous are more than partly to blame! That is exactly where we as the people of God are in these so-called Christian lands of the West in 2014. A colossal removal of Christian principles from national life and society is taking place before our eyes. It is a result of a Satanically energized onslaught on the Inspiration, the Authenticity and the Relevance of God's Word. Sadly as a consequence, there is a collapse of living working faith in many believers.

## A SILENT CHURCH!

We are the witnesses of a church which, for the most part, is silent. Hardly a national leader in the Christian church has spoken up about these matters—same sex marriage, gay rights, and abortion at a very late date when the child is fully formed. Unbelievably, although it is not welcome in evangelical churches, it is only the Catholic Church that has spoken up. Pope John the XXIII was the first, Pope John Paul was the second and Pope Benedict the XVI was the third. They all spoke up against what is happening in so-called Christian nations and their societies. In the preamble to their treatise on European and Anglo-Saxon civilization, the European Commission neither mentioned the Gospel nor the Bible as *the* source or even *a* source. When Pope John Paul requested that they should, they replied, "It is not the preaching of the Gospel nor the Bible which is the source of European and Anglo-Saxon civilization, it is Hellenism," which means Humanism. Then Pope Benedict XVI begged them, "At least put in the preamble that the Gospel and the Bible were *a* source of European and Anglo-Saxon civilization." This time they responded, "It has nothing whatsoever to do with it. Hellenism is the source of our civilization."

## THE CHURCH HAS FAILED

Thank God for the Church in Asia, Africa, and South America where so much is happening and where an emerging church is actually influencing those nations. It is quite extraordinary. Sadly, in the Western so-called Christian nations, there is very largely an apostate church. Where there is a remnant of the faithful, they are often leaderless and just not *activated* but drifting along. If you will allow me to say it, I think the church has failed, and it has failed miserably. There is no excuse whatsoever for the church of God to be in this present situation. We have failed! We have failed in prayer, we have failed in intercession, and we have failed publicly to speak up. Now we are reaping the consequences which we shall see in full measure in the days that lie ahead.

I do not enjoy describing this situation but there is no way out of it. I have never forgotten what Charles Finney wrote in one of his books on awakening and revival. He wrote, "You can always have a revival if there are Christians prepared to pay the price." One of the most extraordinary messages he ever recorded was on *Ploughing up the Fallow Ground*. It is a most uncomfortable message to read as a Christian. He said where there are people prepared day and night to take hold of the Lord, not to be in a fog caused by the confusion around them, but to keep at the matter, it will happen. Where there is such sacrificial intercession and prayer and not a mere mouthing of a few words in a prayer meeting; where there are believers who are *consumed* with a burden conceived by the Holy Spirit until it is fulfilled, then it happens. I think one day when we are in the glory and we hear the full story of every single awakening and revival in the history of the church from the first century until today, we shall hear how it all began with some people prepared to pay the price and become living sacrifices.

## COMFORTABLE CHRISTIANITY

Our Christianity is far too comfortable. We do not want to be disturbed! We want to have the kind of situation in which we have very fine places of worship, wall-to-wall carpeting, ministers of education, ministers of music, ministers for the young, ministers for the old; we want to have a pastor who preaches a message that we can discuss over our Sunday meal, "Wasn't that interesting what the Pastor said this morning?" We do not, however, want *anything* that would turn us upside down, revolutionize us, or challenge us to do something. "Oh, no, no! We do not want anything like that! We do not want to be disturbed. We do not go to church to be disturbed; we go to be what Paul calls *asleep*." We want nothing that would wake us up and challenge us to be involved with the Lord in the fulfillment of His will. Only the Lord can speak to us and save us from this terrible artificial kind of Christianity that we have gotten into. Furthermore, the problem is that the United States which has been in the past a bastion and a bulwark for the preaching of the Gospel, for Biblical truths and principles, has unfortunately exported a kind of church which is not the real church. The result is that the core which is in America, in Britain, in the European and Scandinavian countries, is rotting.

## BE STRONG IN THE LORD

In the Ephesian letter the whole matter is put in simple words. The apostle Paul has been enabled by the Holy Spirit to give us the most extraordinary revelation of God's eternal purpose in this letter. So amazing is what he writes that in chapters one, two, and three, these phrases fall out of the Apostle like a great fountain. One could spend an entire month just thinking about one phrase: "What does it mean?! What is he saying?" It is incredible! There is a statement in Ephesians 3:11 which gives a key to the whole letter: "According to the eternal purpose which He purposed in Christ Jesus our Lord."

When he concludes that letter it is also extraordinary! He concludes it with the words: *Be strong in the Lord and in the strength of His might, put on the whole armor of God that ye may be able to stand.* He writes of the wiles and crafty stratagems of the Devil, and the full power of the forces of evil and darkness launched against us! The key to overcoming is utterly simple. The Lord has provided us with the armor necessary not merely to survive but to triumph and win the battle! That Armor is the Lord Jesus Himself. The second key is to stand, withstand, having done all to stand, and then continue to stand! The extraordinary fact is that we are to stand in the Armor. We need to learn the simple lesson that however furious the battle, we must remain where God by His grace has positioned us. We have to abide and remain abiding in Christ, our Armor.

There are so many ways that the apostle Paul could have finished his letter to the Church in Ephesus. He could have written of the vital necessity of the deepening of the Christian life or of the formation of genuine spiritual character. He could have spoken of the necessity of Bible study, of being in the forefront of prayer, and much else. Instead, he finishes this remarkable letter with the reality that we are in a war and the vital need of being properly clothed for that conflict. If we do not understand what he has written, we will become casualties in this war. No matter how powerful the forces arrayed against the Word of God and the Purpose of God and its fulfillment, He has made full provision for the safety of those whom He has redeemed and for their triumph.

Thus Paul concludes his Ephesian letter in this way:

> Finally, be strong in the Lord, and in the strength of his might. Put on the whole armor of God, that ye may be able to stand against the wiles [or stratagems, strategies] of the devil. For our wrestling is not against flesh and blood, but against the principalities, against the powers, against the world-rulers of this darkness, against the spiritual hosts of wickedness in the heavenly places. Wherefore take up the whole armor of God that ye may be able to withstand in the evil day, and having done all, to stand. Stand therefore. (Ephesians 6:10-14a).

Sadly, the church in Ephesus never listened. We know from the book of Revelation that the Lord said, *You have lost your first love. Unless you remember how far you have fallen and repent and return to your first estate of love and works, I will remove the lampstand from its place* [which is the Testimony of Jesus]; (See Revelation 2:4-5, author's paraphrasing).

We know from history that is an exact description of what happened. The church in Ephesus never repented and never returned to its first love and its first works. The apostle Paul had even prophesied when he left the church of Ephesus for the last time that grievous wolves would enter amongst them not sparing the flock and that men would arise from their midst speaking perverse things and causing divisions (see Acts 20:18-35).

## WE ARE IN A WRESTLING MATCH

It is not the great array of evil spiritual beings that are against the Lord's Word, His work, and His purpose which is the real issue for many genuine believers! The thorny issue and the point at which so many Christian believers stumble is that Paul writes about *wrestling* not with flesh and blood but with those spiritual principalities, powers, world rulers of this present darkness, and hosts of wicked spirits in the heavenlies. To many Christians, this sounds like a fairy tale, at best Star Wars or Battle Star Galactica. To them it is fiction or an illusion, or at the worst delusion. In fact, the Holy Spirit through the apostle Paul reveals that this is not make-believe but **absolute reality**. He is writing out of his own experience. More than most servants of the Lord, he knew those powerful Satanic forces of evil and darkness were intent on snuffing out anything that is the true work of God on this fallen earth. He realized that this wrestling, this struggle with these spiritual forces is a life-long battle for those who are soldiers of the Lord Jesus. Those spiritual principalities and powers know that they cannot harm the Lord Jesus. He has fought the battle and won and has sat down at the right hand of the Father. They cannot dethrone Him nor can they destroy the purpose of the Father for the Lord Jesus. However they can harm the work of God on this fallen earth. They can overcome it, side track it, divide it, and bring false teaching and heresy into it.

For this reason in this ongoing war with these spiritual forces, the Apostle by the Holy Spirit defines the only manner in which we can be safe and we can overcome. When servants of the Lord see spiritual growth and progress in the Church and in believers, it is due to gaining the victory over these powerful evil forces. Where there is weakness, backsliding, apostasy, and departure from the truth, it is due to those forces gaining the victory. In the light of all this, by the Holy Spirit, Paul repeatedly urges us to put on the whole armor of God. I have never yet seen a wrestling match where all the wrestlers were clad in armor. That would be the funniest wrestling match ever seen! J.N. Darby, who sought to be so correct in his translation of the Scriptures, rendered it "for we *struggle* not against flesh and blood but against the principalities," because it is possible that in armor you could struggle but with difficulty. A number of modern versions in English use the word *struggle* for the same reason. Let me put it another way. Paul places a heavy emphasis on being clad with the whole armor and on standing. How do you wrestle and stand at the same time? Have you ever seen a wrestling match? It is a very crude, sweaty vulgar sport in which there can be at least 270 pounds of flesh sitting on another 270 pounds of flesh, or throwing 270 pounds out of the ring. How do you stand and wrestle?

No wonder the later versions say *struggle,* because you can stand and struggle. However the Greek word *palē* is often used in classical Greek when referring to athletes wrestling in either Hellenic or Roman wrestling. It is also used of soldiers in hand-to-hand combat. It seems to me that the English word *wrestling* is correct even if it creates a problem for some. Any servant of God in the forefront of the battle knows that this is not a struggle but a wrestling match. However we know that armor is something you put on. Now I am not just trying to be funny, but one does not cook a meal clad in armor; one does not garden clad in armor; normally one does not take the dog for a walk with armor on. One does not go to bed wearing armor and it would be strange if you had a shower clad in armor. Simply put, armor denotes *war!* It is all to do with combat and conflict! Paul is absolutely right, for we are wrestling with this whole great array of huge spiritual beings. We are only safe when we are fully clothed with the armor of God. That armor is the Lord Jesus. It as simple as that!

### REMAIN WHERE GOD PLACED YOU

Let me put it another way. You remember what the Lord said in John 15: *Abide in Me, and I in you. As the branch cannot bear fruit of itself, except it abide in the vine; so neither can ye, except ye abide in Me...for apart from Me you can do nothing (15:4a; 5b).* When you were saved, God **repositioned** you. He delivered you from the domain of the power of darkness and transferred you into the kingdom of His dear Son (Colossians 1:13). He repositioned you **in Christ**. Remain where God placed you. If you stay where God has placed you, you are absolutely safe and furthermore you will overcome. Overcoming is not something that has to do with very elite and superior people; it is a matter of *position.* If you are in Christ and you abide, or remain and dwell, in Christ, you can do no other but overcome. It is so simple. Why does the apostle Paul write "stand, withstand, having done all to stand and finally stand"? It is the strangest way to win a wrestling match. You do not go backwards, forwards, sideways, left or right; you do not go up, you do not go down; you stand. What does he mean? He means you remain where God the Father has placed you by the Holy Spirit. The day you were born of God and saved by the grace of God, though you may not have even realized it at the time, you were repositioned. Stay where the Father has placed you by the Holy Spirit.

### AN AVALANCHE OF EVIL

In my estimation, we are now certainly facing an avalanche of evil in our nations. Mark my words. It will not just be a flood, but an *avalanche* of evil. You cannot change human society which God has ordained, removing biblical principles which lie at its foundation, without enormous repercussions. Ever since the Gospel was first preached in

18

these lands with tremendous results, biblical truth and principles were placed at the heart of national life. For instance, national society as we know it has been built on the Biblical foundation of one man and one woman coming together in marriage. From that marriage a family was to be produced. If that is changed into same sex marriage and further to that, allowing adoption or having surrogate children, the whole of society will dramatically change within a generation. Is the Lord just going to stand back and smile? It is not only huge changes in society and national life, but in the outlook of the people who constitute those nations. From these dramatic changes, enormous spiritual evil will proceed and flood national life. Everything that the preaching of the Gospel produced in moral and ethical righteousness in national life and character will disappear.

## The Satanic and Powerful Forces Arrayed Against The Lord

The apostle Paul then begins to underline these Satanic and powerful beings and forces which are arrayed against us. We are in an enormous war with the forces of evil and darkness, but we have no need to fear. This battle is the Lords battle and He has provided absolute safety for us in it. If we become casualties it will be our fault and not His. If we become casualties, it will be either our ignorance of the forces against us and the absolute safety we have in the Lord Jesus, or it will be because of our willful disobedience to Him, or because our lives have never been fully surrendered to Him. If we seek to win this battle in our own strength, we will fail and become casualties.

These Satanic forces arrayed against us are:

The Battle of the Ages

## Principalities—Supremos

The Greek word for principalities is archē. This Greek word has passed into English and we see it in archangel, archdeacon, archbishop, architect, architraves, archenemy, archetype and others. What does the apostle Paul mean when he writes: "We wrestle not against flesh and blood but against the principalities"? These principalities are fallen angels—not just any angels—but "supremos." This word archē means chief, first, forerunner, or beginning. I like the word supremo. In other words, they are the top aides to Satan in his affairs and policies and they work for the victory of Satan and the fulfillment of his purpose. It may seem hard for some of us to believe in that possibility. We would think that by now Satan would have realized he has been defeated by God in everything he has ever done. The fact of the matter is however that pride is pride, and Satan still believes that he can win.

## Powers

The word *powers*, *ĕxŏusia* in Greek, means delegated power, competent authority. In other words, these powers are the lower order and they carry out the policies and plans of the Supremos.

## World Rulers of this Darkness

Then there are the "world rulers of this darkness," which means every kind of spiritual darkness from evolutionary theory, Darwinism and such, social darkness, philosophical darkness and religious darkness to name just a few. These are the beings that are particularly specialized in the propagation of this darkness in all its forms.

## *Hosts of Wicked Spirits*

Finally, Paul writes of "hosts of wicked spirits" in the heavenlies. In the Greek it is "wickednesses" and it means wicked spirits. I think the best way to understand this is that they are Satan's civil service in charge of all the practicalities. They are the smaller minions but they are still awful and powerful. They are in charge of overseeing all of Satan's will and work and its execution. They are the kind of spirits that watch your family and find out all its weaknesses and report back to the others on how to trip up your family, your business, the relationship between husband and wife, or how to cause division and faction in the church, and in the work of God. In one sense they are Satan's Intelligence Service. They watch, they spy and they record. Of course, they are spiritually wicked. That is why in Greek they are described as "wickednesses." This is what we face.

## THE ABSOLUTE VICTORY AND TRIUMPH OF THE LORD JESUS

This conflict which the apostle Paul has described in Ephesians 6:10-15 is a war that has its origins from the beginning of creation, before even human beings were created. It is a colossal and ongoing war that began with the rebellion of a third of the angels with Lucifer, Satan as we later know him. Into this confrontation between the Almighty and Satan, we who are the redeemed of God, saved by His grace and born of His Spirit are introduced. The moment God delivered us from the realm of darkness and transferred us into the Kingdom of His dear Son, whether we know it or not, we are the objects of Satan's undying hatred and desire to destroy us, by one means or another!

It was this that Paul understood so clearly and unburdened in Ephesians 6:10-18. It was not only the huge

21

battle that the redeemed of God are in which he describes, but also the absolute means by which we can endure the conflict and win the victory. The secret is to always to be clad in the **whole** Armor of God which is the Messiah Jesus, and to stand, withstand, and having done all to stand in Him. Upon what are we standing? We are standing on the foundation of His finished work, on His Word, and on His will.

The simple fact is mind blowing! Jesus the Messiah has won the victory and totally beaten the forces of evil and death. He has sat down at the right hand of the Father, seated until all of His enemies are placed under His feet (see Psalm 110). When we declare that Jesus has won and is enthroned at the right hand of God the Father, the forces of evil and darkness are rendered powerless! We are using the sword of the Spirit which is the Word of God. Satan cannot dethrone Him, nor paralyze Him, nor lessen His total triumph one whit. Satan and his host can do a war dance around those saved and born of God, but it is when we are clad in the Armor and standing in the Lord Jesus, that they are rendered powerless!

# Chapter Two

## THIS WORLD IS ESSENTIALLY SPIRITUAL

I beheld till thrones were placed, and one that was ancient of days did sit: his raiment was white as snow, and the hair of his head like pure wool; his throne was fiery flames and wheels thereof burning fire. A fiery stream issued and came forth from before him: thousands of thousands ministered unto him, and ten thousand times ten thousand stood before him: the judgement was set, and the books were opened..... I saw in the night-visions and, behold, there came with the clouds of heaven one like unto a son of man, and he came even to the ancient of days, and they brought him near before him. And there was given him dominion, and glory, and a kingdom, that all the peoples, nations, and languages should serve him: his dominion is an everlasting dominion, which shall not pass away, and his kingdom that which shall not be destroyed. (Daniel 7:9-10; 13-14)

And when the servant of the man of God was risen early, and gone forth, behold, a host with horses and chariots was round about the city. And his servant said unto him, Alas, my master! how shall we do? And he answered, Fear not; for they that are with us are more than they that are with them. And Elisha prayed, and said, LORD, I pray thee, open his eyes, that he may see. And the Lord opened the eyes of the young man; and he saw: and, behold, the mountain was full of horses and chariots of fire round about Elisha. (2 Kings 6:15-17)

And I saw in the right hand of him that sat on the throne a book written within and on the back, close sealed with seven seals. And I saw a strong angel proclaiming with a great voice, Who is worthy to open the book, and to loose the seals thereof? And no one in the heaven, or on the earth, or under the earth, was able to open the book, or to look thereon. And I wept much, because no one was found worthy to open the book, or to look thereon: and one of the elders saith unto me, Weep not; behold, the Lion that is of the tribe of Judah, the Root of David, hath overcome to open the book and the seven seals thereof. And I saw in the midst of the throne and of the four living creatures, and in the midst of the elders, a Lamb standing, as though it had been slain. (Revelation 5:1-6)

Unto me, who am less than the least of all saints, was this grace given, to preach unto the Gentiles the unsearchable riches of Christ; and to make all men see what is the dispensation of the mystery which for ages hath been hid in God who created all things; to the intent that now unto the principalities and the powers in the heavenly places might be made known through the church the manifold wisdom of God, according to the eternal purpose which he purposed in Christ Jesus our Lord. (Ephesians 3:8-11)

Wherefore we faint not; but though our outward man is decaying, yet our inward man is renewed day by day. For our light affliction, which is for the moment, worketh for us more and more exceedingly an eternal weight of glory; while we look not at the things which are seen, but the things that are not seen: for the things which are seen are temporal; but the things which are not seen are eternal. (2 Corinthians 4:16-18)

## THE SPIRITUAL WORLD IN WHICH WE AS THE REDEEMED LIVE

These Scriptures, with which we have introduced this chapter, reveal that once we are truly born of the Spirit of God, we have been ushered into a spiritual dimension. By that new birth, the Lord has given us the spiritual ability to know and see the Lord and to hear and understand Him. The apostle Paul in fact prayed that the believers in Ephesus might "have the eyes of their heart enlightened that they might know what is the hope of his calling, what are the riches of the glory of His inheritance in the Saints, and what is the exceeding greatness of his power to usward who believe" (Ephesians 1:18-19). The Lord Jesus Himself said: "My sheep hear my voice, and I know them and they follow me" (John 10:27). When we see and hear the Lord, no matter what the conditions or circumstances in which we are found, we grow in the grace and knowledge of our Lord and Savior, Jesus the Messiah. This knowledge is not merely academic or theological, important as that may be; it is an intimate, firsthand experience of the Lord, a daily walk with Him.

### "LORD, OPEN HIS EYES THAT HE MAY SEE"

In 2 Kings 6:8-23, we have the incredible story of the Prophet Elisha's servant. The fact that this young man lived with Elisha, served Elisha, and traveled with him voluntarily, seems to indicate that he was a faithful believer. However, like many genuine believers he had physical eyes and ears, but the eyes and ears of his spirit were not activated.

Apparently, the king of Syria suspected that someone in his retinue was an Israeli spy because everything he said and did the Prophet Elisha knew and relayed the information to the king of Israel. Of course this was before the days of radio, telephones, iPads, and bugging equipment! When the king of Syria said that whoever was spying would be arrested, one of his servants said, "Do you not know that whatever you secretly say in your bedroom, the Israeli Prophet Elisha knows and passes it on to the king of Israel?" The king

25

of Syria reacted: "We will put an end to it." He ordered that detachments of his army immediately be sent to bring Elisha back captive.

In the morning whilst Elisha's servant was preparing Elisha's breakfast, he thought he saw movement out of the window. To his surprise, when he looked closer, he saw a number of Syrian soldiers. He then went to another window and saw more, and yet more from another window. He realized that the house was surrounded by the Syrian army, and he panicked. In a terrible state of fear, he fled to Elisha and said, "We are surrounded, whatever shall we do?" Elisha did not even sit his servant down and speak about his need to have faith; nor did he reprimand him for being overcome with fear. Instead, he made a statement of calm faith and said, "Fear not; for they that are with us are more than they that are with them." I am not sure that this helped his terrified servant. Elisha then prayed the shortest prayer in the Bible: "Lord, I pray thee, open his eyes that he may see." In a single moment of time, the young man saw the mountain covered with horses and chariots of fire. It was the host, the armies, of the Lord!

That young man had physical eyes and he had used them. He saw the Syrian army surrounding Elisha's home and he panicked and was filled with terror. There was no point in Elisha counseling him to have faith. What he did not see with those eyes were the armies of the Lord surrounding the Syrians. The result was amazing. Elisha and his servant led the whole Syrian army detachment blind to the king of Israel. That heavenly host was there from the moment the army detachment had moved from Syria, but Elisha's servant could not see them. The Spiritual eyes of his spirit were not open. I imagine that young man was never the same again. He had seen that this world is essentially a spiritual world.

The lesson which Elisha's servant learned is a vitally strategic lesson that all genuine believers need to learn! A living and practical faith is born in a child of God when he or she spiritually sees and hears the Lord. Without such spiritual sight and hearing, we are left only with the physical circumstances and problems which appear insurmountable.

### ENDURING AS SEEING HIM WHO IS INVISIBLE

The writer of the Hebrew letter clearly states, speaking of Moses that, *By Faith he forsook Egypt, not fearing the wrath of the king: for he endured, as seeing him who is invisible"* (Hebrews 11:27). The point that the writer makes by the Holy Spirit is that Moses was able to endure everything because he saw "Him who is invisible." He did not see everything as it was physically to do with time and sense, but he saw through to that eternal world. In fact he wrote that Moses:

> Refused to be called the son of Pharaoh's daughter; choosing rather to share ill treatment with the people of God, than to enjoy the pleasures of sin for a season; accounting the reproach of *the* Christ [mg] greater riches than the treasures of Egypt: for he looked unto the recompense of reward. (Hebrews 11:24b-26)

It would have been impossible for a prince of Egypt, a grandson of Pharaoh, to account all the wealth, power, and influence of the greatest super power of the day as nothing compared with the reproach of the Messiah, and to being part of the people of the Messiah.

It was because he endured "as seeing Him who is invisible." Only a child of God who has his or her eyes opened to see Him who is invisible could so act, so choose, and so live!

If this physical world is essentially a spiritual world, the only way to overcome in it is by spiritual means. The apostle Paul wrote:

> For though we walk in the flesh, we do not war according to the flesh (for the weapons of our warfare are not of the flesh, but mighty before God, to the casting down of strongholds). (2 Corinthians 10:3-4)

All these weapons are spiritual and can only be exercised "before God," in the presence of the Lord. For example, the Apostle wrote that we are to take the Sword of the Spirit which is the Word of God, following what he wrote about wrestling with principalities and powers, and the need to put on the whole armor of God which is Christ. The weapons of our warfare, the sword of the Spirit, and the armor that we are to put on are all spiritual matters.

## SEEING THE DIVINE
## BEHIND PHYSICAL WORLD HISTORY

Even the most simple and shallow reading of the Bible, would bring us to the conclusion that those called the Redeemed within its pages, see and hear the Lord. The Lord is the center and circumference of their life and existence. They walk with the Lord, and they experience Him. Wherever we turn within the Word of God, we find men and women saved by His grace who see the whole course of human history, both its fallen, dark, and evil aspect and God's merciful intention to overcome it, until the final fulfillment of His purpose.

After all the Bible begins with the fall of man, traces the human story and Satan's never-ending desire to preempt the purpose of God; at the same point, the promise of redemption and salvation is made within its first chapters (Genesis 3:15). That salvation would be through "the seed of the woman," and its realization through the finished work of the Messiah Jesus on Calvary. The promised redemption would end in the Eternal Glory of God.

With Abraham it began when the God of glory appeared to him, and he saw within the glory of God, the City of God's glory. In one sense from the moment he was saved, he saw through thousands of years to the New Jerusalem coming down out of heaven having the Glory of God (see Revelation chapter 21-22). It is said of Abraham: *For he looked for the city which hath the foundations, whose builder and maker is God* (Hebrews 11:10.) Of whom else should I speak? Of Daniel, who saw the whole course of history from his day until the first coming of the Messiah, and His return at the end of time? Shall I mention Isaiah or Jeremiah or Ezekiel, and many more of the prophets? They saw the physical history of empires and nations as being in some way centered in the coming of the Messiah Jesus. The apostle John saw the whole course of history from his day until the return of the Messiah in glory. If you look through the Apocalypse (Revelation), note how many times John says "I saw." His feet were on this fallen earth, in fact in a Roman forced labor camp on Patmos, but his eyes were on the Lion of Judah, the little Lamb as it had been slain in the midst of God's throne. He saw the Lord Jesus as the key to physical history. Shall I write of the apostle Paul who through all of his

29

tribulations and sufferings had his eyes fixed on Jesus, the author and finisher of his faith? We owe so much to those who by faith and patience endured and ministered to us the Word of God. Paul saw so clearly the whole purpose of God and the stages of its fulfillment through history, until the final ingathering of the Gentile believers and the salvation of the Jewish people. These are but a few examples of those who by their walk with God, although on this earth and very human, entered into a spiritual dimension of seeing and of understanding the Lord.

## HISTORY IS THE EXPRESSION OF INVISIBLE SPIRITUAL BEINGS

All human history is the expression of Spiritual forces and beings. For many people such a dogmatic statement is ridiculous! This world for such people is merely and only to do with time and sense. Apparently, we got onto this planet by evolving from primeval slime or something akin to it. The planet itself just happened, probably through some cosmic explosion! According, however, to the Word of God, the greatest factor is what is eternal! Buried in the book of the preacher is one extraordinary word: *He hath made everything beautiful in its time: also he hath set eternity in their heart, yet so that man cannot find out the work that God hath done from the beginning even to its end* (Ecclesiastes 3:11). Man can fill himself with human wisdom and philosophy, with pursuing a career, building a great business empire, with sport, with sex, or other pleasures, but nothing ever satisfies. Simply stated, it is the problem of *eternity in the heart*.

The greatest factor in this world of time and sense is God Himself. It is the Eternal One who has neither beginning nor end. The Bible begins with the incredibly simple statement: "In the beginning God" (Genesis 1:1). The apostle John wrote: "In the beginning was the Word, and the Word was with God, and the Word was God" (John 1:1). The Lord Jesus speaking of Satan said: "Now is the judgment of this world; now shall the prince of this world be cast out (John 12:31). The Messiah was speaking of His death on the Cross and the expulsion of Satan through it. All these matters are spiritual facts that have to be discerned by the revelation of the Holy Spirit. The apostle Paul stated it simply: *But the natural man does not receive the things of the Spirit of God; for they are foolishness to him; nor can he know them, because they are spiritually discerned* (1 Corinthians 2:14 NKJV).

All of world history is the expression of this cosmic battle between God and his unfallen and loyal angels on the one hand, and Satan and his fallen, dark and evil spiritual beings on the other. It is possible that some who read this little book cannot agree with what I am writing. However, I firmly believe that all of history is the expression of both fallen and unfallen invisible beings. The fallen angels have sought to fulfill the will of Satan and worked evil, darkness, and iniquity through willing human beings. At the same time, the loyal hosts of the Lord have sought to fulfill His work and will do so through redeemed human beings, indwelt by the Lord Jesus through the Holy Spirit. Those who have surrendered to the Lordship of Jesus have stood throughout history for His throne to touch this fallen earth that His will be done in it, although it is fallen.

The Battle of the Ages

From the Word of God, we know very well that
there is coming a time when "the man of sin" will be
revealed. This will be an evil day *par excellence*. How
near we are to that we do not know. It is possible that
we are nearer than we think (2 Thessalonians 2:3-4 cp
v. 7). What is "the power that restrains" the coming of
the man of sin? There have been many suggestions,
ranging from the rapture of the Saints, to the taking of
the Holy Spirit out of the world! In my estimation, the
traditional Jewish view is right that there are great
Archangels who uphold law and order, righteousness,
and justice, and who also restrain evil and disorder. If I
may put it yet another way, there are fallen angelic
beings who seek to control and dominate human
history, who are kept in check by the Archangels of
God until the time comes when the Almighty
withdraws them.

## THE LOYAL HOSTS OF GOD

These powerful, loyal, unfallen spiritual beings are
the great principalities, the princes, the Archangels who
stand for the success of the work of God and for the
fulfillment of the will of God. They have watched over
what the Lord Jesus has launched into being and have
continued to watch over its course until sometimes a
whole nation is transformed (see Matthew 16:18). That
is what happened with the moving of the Holy Spirit
which resulted at different times in the Quakers, the
Puritans and the Covenanters. It also happened with the
Anabaptists, the Moravians, and with the First Great
Evangelical Awakening led by Wesley and Whitfield.
Millions found the Lord! Even that silly old king who
lost the Colonies in America through his stupidity,
ordered by decree three days of mourning when John

Wesley died, and stipulated that he should be buried in Westminster Abbey.

When those great movements took place, it resulted in multitudes of people being saved and transformed and who were by the Holy Spirit brought into a living union with the Lord Jesus. They believed in the Bible and in the truth of the gospel, and as a result, biblical Principles were set at the heart of those nations. These Biblical Principles became the foundation of their national life and society. Whether it was to do with service for or to the nation, or family and marriage—all that we take for granted—they all came out of those awakenings. Harsh and evil matters were reformed; consider child reform. They used to send little boys up to clean out chimneys which resulted in their early death. This was practiced until the Christians with a single voice called on Parliament to stop such child abuse and labor. Nursing began with the Quakers such as Florence Nightingale, and others. The great prison reforms began with Elizabeth Frye who was another Quaker and other Christians. All these things resulted from the movements of the Holy Spirit. Surely we know that in American history there were successive awakenings and revivals which through the Grace of God came through people like Jonathan Edwards and many others, and swept over what were then called the Colonies. God changed the hearts of the people. This also happened in the Netherlands and in Germany before Nazism, with the great Reformation led by Martin Luther. It happened in the Scandinavian countries of Norway, Sweden, Finland, and Denmark. Everywhere we look we see the same incredible picture and result. Nations were changed for the better. When the Lord saved people, He gave them a new and tender heart of love to change what was wrong in society and to overcome evil with love.

None of these matters can be seen with the natural eye or be understood by the natural mind. No natural eye can see Jesus at the right hand of God; no natural mind can understand that in building His church, and preserving it when it is in danger of backsliding, He launches these initiatives of the Holy Spirit. A believer who is spiritually alive will realize that this world is essentially a spiritual world. That which is eternal is spiritual; all else decays and dies. The prophet Elisha's servant, whose eyes were opened in a moment of panic and distress, discovered that behind this world of time and sense, there is a spiritual world which is eternal.

The apostle Paul writing to the church at Corinth wrote of matters that cannot be properly understood unless one sees the eternal world (see 2 Corinthians 4:16-18). He writes of *our light affliction which is working for us more and more exceedingly an eternal weight of glory* (2 Corinthians 4:17). Such a statement is ludicrous for the man of the world or the child of God who does not see and understand the eternal world. Affliction that is light, working for us an eternal weight of Glory, seems nonsensical! However, Paul explains himself: *While we look not at the things which are seen, but at the things which are not seen: for things which are seen are temporal; but the things which are not seen are eternal* (2 Corinthians 4:18).

### THE UNFALLEN ANGELS HAVE BEEN DISLODGED

It seems to me that the good principalities, the unfallen angelic principalities, have been dislodged by the evil ones. Nothing else could cause this incredible avalanche of paganism in the Western Nations, and the speed with which it is taking place. You will remember the Prince of Persia and the Prince of Greece as recorded in the book of Daniel (10:10-21). These were not human Princes but powerful Spiritual Beings. Gabriel, an Archangel, was expressly sent by God to Daniel with a message saying: "God heard you the moment that you started to intercede and is going to answer." On the way, Gabriel said that he got into a fight which lasted twenty one days, but the Archangel Michael came to his aid. Is all of this a fairytale or a legend? Both the Prince of Persia and the Prince of Greece, the Archangels Michael and Gabriel are all Spiritual Beings who cannot normally be seen with the naked eye. It is a window into a spiritual world, which has far more effect on the physical world then most of us realize.

I believe that those great archangels or supremos were originally watching over the British Empire and its growth as it became the largest single factor in the gospel being preached throughout the whole world. I think of the United States and that archangel who has watched over its development, its Constitution, and of everything which is good in American life, in particular, the manner in which the United States became a bastion of biblical truth and a center for the propagation of the Gospel worldwide.

It seems to me that those good unfallen angels have been dislodged. One of the reasons is that the church has never helped them by standing for the whole truth as it is in Jesus. It has not heeded the divine call to genuine intercession, to stand for the truth of God's Word, and for His will to be done in this fallen world whatever its condition. The apostle Paul clearly states it is God's intention that through the Church His manifold wisdom might be made known to principalities and powers in the heavenlies (see Ephesians 3:8-11). It is exactly here that the Church has failed. Sadly, it is a fact that part of the Church has become and is becoming apostate, questioning whether the Word of God *is* the Word of God and even relevant to the twenty first century.

In the present situation which we are facing, the prophetic warning which the apostle Paul gave to the church in Ephesus, one of the finest assemblies in the New Testament era, becomes incredibly relevant. He wrote that we are not wrestling against flesh and blood, matters of people or of time and sense, but against principalities, powers, world rulers of this darkness, and hosts of wicked spirits in the heavenlies. For this reason, the Apostle emphasizes the need to put on the whole Armor of God which is the Lord Jesus Himself. However fierce the battle, we are absolutely safe if we stand, withstand, and continue to stand in Christ.

## A SERIOUS WORD OF WARNING

There are three serious warnings that need to be made and underlined:

### *The First Warning:*

It is possible when as the redeemed we begin to realize that we live in a spiritual world, to become unhealthily demon conscious! We then find "demons under every cushion." Everything is demonic, not only in the world at large, but even in our personal and family circumstances. The result is instead of our eyes being on the Lord Jesus and our lives being Christ centered and positive, we become negative and depressed. It is, however, a huge step forward to become aware of the spiritual and demonic forces that we as believers face. It is nevertheless possible to become paranoid and not experience the absolute victory that is ours in the Lord Jesus. The fact is that Jesus has won. He has triumphed over Satan and all these spiritual and demonic forces. The apostle Paul wrote:

> Giving thanks unto the Father, who made us meet to be partakers of the inheritance of the Saints in light; who delivered us out of the power of darkness, and translated us into the kingdom of the Son of his love; in whom we have our redemption... (Colossians 1:12-14)

We, who are saved by the grace of God, have been delivered from the power of darkness and transferred into the kingdom of His Son, in whom we have been redeemed.

## *The Second Warning:*

In powerful intercession and prayer warfare, it is possible to be carried away by our flesh and emotion and uncover ourselves. That is exactly what the forces of evil and darkness want. They can then knock us out of the battle and make us casualties. We must not imagine that because we are in the armor of God, we can seek to belittle those principalities and powers, calling them names, and railing against them. If we are truly abiding in Christ, in God's armor, we will know the Holy Spirit restraining us from taking such action.

We must always remember the warning that Jude gives us in Jude 8-10. When battling with these principalities we need to remember that the Archangel

Michael dared not to bring a railing accusation against Satan but said the Lord rebuke you Satan. It is never wise to speak directly with these principalities and powers. I have seen in my own life and experience many spiritual casualties as a result of deriding, belittling, and holding up to ridicule such spiritual beings. Of course, I am not writing about the deliverance of people from demonic possession, in which spirits need to be commanded in the name of Jesus to come out of them.

Nevertheless, we who are saved and justified by the grace of God have absolutely no reason to fear! God has provided us with not only the armor, which is Christ, but also with the weapons through which the enemies of God can be thrown down and their works destroyed. We gain the victory in this confrontation with the Forces of Evil and Darkness by proclaiming and declaring the total victory of the Lord Jesus. He is Lord over everything and is enthroned at the Father's right hand. There is no way whatsoever that Satan with his principalities and cohorts can dethrone Him. In fact, God the Father has said of the Lord Jesus that He is to sit at His right hand until He makes all His enemies His footstool.

There is no reason to have a conversation, let alone a slanging match with these Principalities and Powers. It is the Truth that paralyzes them and renders them impotent. When the Word of God, the Truth of God which is Jesus (John 14:6) is proclaimed and declared, we overcome the forces of darkness however powerful they seem to be.

This is the enormous value in spiritual warfare of praise and worship, the proclamation and declaration of the Truth. Is Jesus Lord? Is he enthroned at the right hand of the Father? Is all Authority and Power in heaven and on this fallen earth committed by the Father into the hands of the Lord Jesus? If so, these are spiritually nuclear weapons!!! The Spiritual forces arrayed against us are silenced, disarmed, and overcome when we proclaim and enforce the total victory of the Lord Jesus over them.

### *The Third Warning:*

Once we as believers have our spiritual eyes opened to the reality of a good and heavenly angelic order, the Evil One can push us to extremes. Instead of Christ being the center and circumference of our lives, in a wrong and dangerous manner we can become "angel conscious." The Word of God expressly declares that these unfallen angels are "all ministering spirits, sent forth to do service for the sake of them that shall inherit salvation" (Hebrews 1:14). Most believers are unaware of the tremendous ministry that these angels perform toward them, to their families, to the church, and to the work of God. Those angels never bring attention to themselves but always to the Lord Jesus, to His enthronement, and to His absolute triumph.

The apostle Paul wrote the letter to the Colossians because one of the heresies, amongst others, which was making inroads in that fellowship of believers was a far too great attention being given to the angelic world. He even wrote of the "worshiping of the angels" (see Colossians 2:18-19). For this reason, the Colossian letter emphasizes the centrality and sufficiency of the Lord Jesus. The whole creation was created through Him and for Him. He is the beginning and the end of salvation. He is the head of the church which is His body. *In Him dwelleth all the fullness of the Godhead bodily and in Him ye are made full, who is the head of all principality and power* (Colossians 2:9-10). When our spiritual eyes have been opened to a spiritual world, our total safety depends upon our giving to the Lord Jesus the place which God the Father has given Him.

# Chapter Three

## THE WORD OF GOD AND THE
## TESTIMONY OF JESUS

That which the palmer-worm hath left hath the locust eaten; and that which the locust hath left hath the canker-worm eaten; and that which the canker-worm hath left hath the caterpillar eaten. (Joel 1:4)

Blow the trumpet in Zion, sanctify a fast, call a solemn assembly; gather the people, sanctify the assembly, assemble the old men, gather the children, and those that suck the breasts; let the bridegroom go forth from his chamber, and the bride out of her closet. Let the priests, the ministers of the Lord, weep between the porch and the altar, and let them say, Spare thy people, O Lord, and give not thy heritage to reproach, that the nations should rule over them: wherefore should they say among the peoples, Where is their God? (Joel 2:15-17)

I John, your brother and partaker with you in the tribulation and kingdom and patience *which are* in Jesus, was in the isle that is called Patmos, for the word of God and the testimony of Jesus. (Revelation 1:9)

### THE ONSLAUGHT OF UNBELIEF AND DARKNESS

The Prophet Joel as recorded in Joel chapter one, perfectly describes our present condition. We are watching everything being destroyed. It is the destruction and discarding of all that which was placed with great cost at the heart of our national life, whether it is in the States, in the European nations, or in Britain. Martyrs shed their blood, others gave life-long and sacrificial service, and yet others faced every kind of violent opposition to bring to us the living Word of God in our mother tongue. The constitution placed at the heart of our nations, which ensured our freedom and personal rights, embodied biblical truth and principles. Those biblical principles are now secretly being destroyed. Like the silent work of the palmer-worm, the locust, the canker worm, and the caterpillar, all is being eaten away and destroyed. It is a perfect description of the ongoing paganization of the Western nations.

How shall we who are the redeemed people of God face this situation? It is a timely and vitally strategic question. The Church at large seems to be complacent, drifting along with the tide of the world. Apostasy is eating into the life of the Church and rendering her unable to withstand or even to speak up against this onslaught of unbelief and darkness. Even where there are companies and fellowships of believers who are seeking to be faithful, they seem powerless to do anything! Amongst some, there is a readiness "to throw in the towel" and "call it a day." They believe that if the Lord Jesus prophetically described this falling away of believers, this apostasy of the Church in the last days, we can do nothing whatsoever about it. The last book of the Bible deals with this very subject. In all the apostasy of the Church, the paganization of society, and the rampant power of evil, there are the overcomers on every page. They by the blood of the Lamb have overcome. They never denied in any shape or form the Word of God and the Testimony of Jesus. *These are they who follow the Lamb whithersoever He goeth* (Revelation 14:4).

## THE WORD OF GOD AND THE TESTIMONY OF JESUS

When the apostle John was detained on Patmos by Imperial Rome, he wrote that it was for the Word of God and the Testimony of Jesus. Throughout the twenty-two chapters of the book of Revelation, we discover this theme. In all the cataclysmic judgments described throughout this book, the violent wars and huge confrontation between God and his own and Satan and his own, we discover these overcoming believers who are faithful to the Word of God and the Testimony of Jesus.

It begins with an incredible vision into that spiritual world which lies behind the physical world. We see the Lion of Judah, the little Lamb as it had been slain, enthroned at the heart of the universe with all sovereign power and authority both in heaven and on this fallen earth committed by God the Father into His hands. It ends with the New Jerusalem coming down out of heaven, having the Glory of God. That City of God is described as the bride and the wife of the Lamb. The battle has finally been won and the purpose of God gloriously fulfilled.

It is interesting to note the link which the Holy Spirit makes between the Testimony of Jesus and the Word of God. Jesus is the Word of God incarnate. John stated it simply when he wrote in the beginning of his Gospel: *And the Word became flesh, and dwelt among us (and we beheld His glory, glory as of the only begotten of the Father), full of grace and truth* (John 1:14). Jesus is the heart and mind of God articulated or verbalized. He is the revelation of who God is, and through Him we come to a living knowledge of God. Twice in the Apocalypse, the book of Revelation, Jesus proclaims that He is the Alpha and the Omega (Revelation 1:8 and 22:13). The Lord Jesus is the Alphabet of God, the "A" and "Z" and all the letters in between! Simply stated, it means if God says anything or reveals Himself in any way it is through the Messiah Jesus. He is the articulation of the Truth of God.

When the Lord Jesus spoke to the seven churches, every one of them was represented by a seven branched lampstand, the menorah. That lampstand in the Tabernacle and Temple was the only means of physical light. The basic significance of that lampstand is that the Lord Jesus is the light of God (see John 8:12 cp 1 Thessalonians 5:4-5; Matthew 5:14-16). It is clear, however, that this Light of God is to shine through the Church. In the same manner in which the seven branched Lampstand holds the seven oil lamps alight, the Church must hold the Testimony of Jesus. If the world is to see God, the Church must hold the Testimony of Jesus! The churches are meant to be the vessels through which the light of God shines into the darkness of this world.

### DWELLING IN THE HOUSE OF THE LORD

The vision which the Prophet Zechariah had, as recorded in Zechariah chapter 4, is of the utmost importance to our understanding of this matter. It was all to do with the rebuilding of the destroyed house of God in his day. He and the other faithful believers who were with him were facing every kind of satanic opposition and tribulation. The problems confronting the builders were seemingly mountainous and insurmountable! Then God gave him the vision of the golden seven branched lampstand of the Tabernacle and Temple. When Zechariah asked the angel of God what it was all about, the angel said:

> This is the Word of the Lord unto Zerubbabel saying, not by might, nor by power, but by My Spirit saith the Lord of hosts. He went on to say, Who art thou O great mountain? Before Zerubbabel thou shalt become a plain: and he shall bring forth the top stone with shoutings of Grace, grace unto it. (Zechariah 4:6-7)

In Zechariah's day, the Temple, the house of God, symbolized the dwelling place of God. The Almighty has longed from the beginning to dwell amongst the redeemed. This explains how everything in the Old Testament (or Covenant) is centered in the Temple. For Example, in Psalm 132, the Lord expresses this desire: *For the Lord hath chosen Zion; He hath desired it for his habitation. This is my resting-*

*place forever: Here will I dwell; for I have desired it* (Psalm 132:13-14).

In Psalm 87 it is written: *His foundation is in the holy mountains. The Lord loveth the gates of Zion more than all the dwellings of Jacob. Glorious things are spoken of thee, O city of God* (Psalm 87:1-3). In a very real sense this little Psalm of seven verses encapsulates the whole eternal purpose of God. After all, why does He say, *His foundation is in the holy mountains*? There is no meaning to a foundation unless something is built on it. It is the house of the Lord that has to be built on it! All through both the Old Testament and the New Testament, we discover this longing of God. In the Old Testament, everything is judged by its relationship to the house of God in Jerusalem. For example we have in I and II Kings where every king was judged on his relationship to the Temple and I and II Chronicles which records the faithfulness or unfaithfulness of the nation as regards the Temple.

In the New Testament, the apostle Paul states it simply and clearly:

> Having been built upon the foundation of the apostles and prophets, Christ Jesus Himself being the corner stone, in whom the whole building, being fitted together is growing into a holy temple in the Lord; in whom you also are being built together into a dwelling of God in the Spirit. (Ephesians 2:20-22 NASB)

The apostle Peter also expresses the same truth:

> Unto whom coming, a living stone, rejected indeed of men, but with God elect, precious, ye also, as living stones, are built up a spiritual house, to be a holy priesthood, to offer up spiritual sacrifices acceptable to God through Jesus Christ. Because it is contained in scripture, Behold I lay in Zion a chief corner stone, elect, precious: And he that believeth on him shall not be put to shame. (1 Peter 2:4-6)

We need to note the enormous emphasis in the New Testament on being "built up" or "built together." It is summed up in the words: "let all things be done unto building up." The bottom line is that it is to do with being part of the house of God, the dwelling place and home of the Lord. The Testimony of Jesus has much to do with the house of the Lord as the home of God.

## THE TESTIMONY OF JESUS

Therefore, if the world is to hear Him, we need to be the body through which the Head speaks and expresses Himself. In the first verses of the book of Acts, Luke says: *I have written the former treatise, O Theophilus, concerning all that Jesus began both to do and to teach until the day in which He was received up* (Acts 1:1-2). Note carefully the words *began both to do and to teach*. The book of Acts was the continuation of the Lord Jesus revealing and expressing Himself through His body, firstly to the Jewish people, then to the Samaritans, and then to the Gentiles.

It is the kind of church where sinners and prostitutes feel strangely at home, although lost in evil and sin. They have a witness within their dead spirit: "I have come home; God is here." I Corinthians 14:25 tells us of a person who fell down on his face in a meeting of the church and said, "God is here." Every human being has within them that homing instinct. It is explained by that which is written in Ecclesiastes: *He hath set eternity in their heart* (Ecclesiastes 3:11). When the church is what it ought to be, the body of the Lord Jesus of which He is head, it becomes the home of God. Every person who comes into that church, when it gathers, senses they have touched something which is not of the world but is of God. Even though they are unsaved, the Spirit of God prompts something in them deep within their dead spirit: "You have come home."

It was that way when Jesus was on the earth. The publicans and sinners sat with him, drank with him, ate with him, and laughed with him, much to the upset of the religious!

46

They could not understand how publicans and sinners, prostitutes, lepers, and social outcasts were irresistibly and irretrievably drawn to Him. That is the Testimony of Jesus! The Lord Jesus was not only the Mind of God revealed, He was also the Heart of God revealed.

I was once in a company where many of the folks, especially the sisters, did not even know what tobacco smoke smelled like. They were so separated from the world that in the course of their lives, they had totally separated from unsaved human beings. They had no idea what was going on outside their company of believers. The Testimony of Jesus is so amazing. At one time a Pharisee asked Jesus to come to his home and have a meal with him. A woman who was a known prostitute in the city stood behind Jesus weeping. She wet the feet of Jesus with her tears then wiped them with her hair and kissed them. Finally, she anointed His feet with a precious ointment. The Pharisee host who saw it was horrified thinking: "If He was a truly holy man, he would have surely realized what kind of woman this is" (Luke 7:37-39). It is extraordinary that this sinful woman was irretrievably drawn to Jesus who was the Word of God incarnate. One would have thought that she would have avoided Him at all costs, especially in a Pharisee's home. That, however, is the Testimony of Jesus. Of course, that does not mean that we condone sin or encourage it; it means that sinners have finally found their home. That home is in Jesus. It is as simple as that. Her touching Jesus, washing His feet and anointing them did not make the Lord Jesus less holy. It did something for that fallen and sinful woman. This shows how far away we are in our understanding of the Church, considering it as a routine, a ritual, a cold, hard, and legalistic place. What I have said is summed up in a couplet written by C.T. Studd:

# The Battle of the Ages

*Some want to live within the sound*
*Of chapel chime or bell*
*I'd rather run a rescue shop*
*Within a yard of Hell!*

May the Lord touch our hearts and help us. We are facing a collapse in the United States and in other Western nations which were once termed "Christian." It is my personal conviction that it is the judgment of the Lord on these nations. God is allowing it because of our half-heartedness as Christians. This assault is clear; it is on the Word of God and the Testimony of Jesus. The only answer is a people prepared to lay down their lives in intercession who will pray until God moves in power. It will take our whole being: spirit, soul and body. It will require believers who will meet together, discovering what is His will for this situation and who will seek Him continuously until He answers.

## FAILURE TO ENFORCE THE WILL OF GOD

God is very much interested in training us in intercession. That training is not "a bed of roses," it requires discipline, sacrifice, and time. It also requires the spiritual faculties within us that came through our spiritual birth to be trained. Those faculties of hearing and of seeing need to be tuned, sensitized, and sharpened to Him. He is training us to be in touch with the throne of God and how to enforce the will of God. When the Lord gave us "the pattern prayer," He taught us to pray *Thy kingdom come, Thy will be done as in heaven, so on earth* (Matthew 6:10 as in the Greek). He is not teaching us to pray that in some **far distant future** the kingdom of God will come and the will of God be done. In the whole of the pattern prayer He gave us, it is in the present. Our Father **who art** in Heaven (that is present); Hallowed be thy Name (present), give us this day our daily bread; forgive us our trespasses (all in the present). It is in this that we have failed. The Church is meant to be light in darkness. Much of it through its apostasy is now darkness in darkness—maybe not completely, but very largely. When we have an evangelical in Britain planning a marriage service for same-sex couples, or another Bishop who at one time said that the resurrection of Jesus is a cheap conjuring trick with bones, we know we have come to an end. We have another Bishop saying that Jesus had a sexual liaison with Mary Magdalene. Where does he get it? We had yet another who said that Jesus was gay. It is unbelievable. The Church is supposed to be light in darkness, to be salt halting the corruption. It is meant to be a city set on a hill which everybody can see, holding forth the Word of Life. Supremely the Church is meant to hold the Testimony of Jesus. When the Church is what it should be, Jesus lives again through His body on this fallen earth and powerfully expresses Himself. Sadly, much of the Church is far away from being what it should be.

## THE SUPREME BATTLE OF OUR AGE

The enormous and persistent battle of this age is over the Word of God and the Testimony of Jesus. When the glorified Messiah poured out the Holy Spirit on the festival of Shavuot (or Pentecost) at the beginning of this age, this furious battle began. The aim of Satan and his powerful cohorts was simple! It was to compromise the Word of God by diluting it with other material from this world's philosophy, fashion, and outlook. Every kind of heresy concerning the Word of God and the person of Jesus was developed. From that point onwards throughout history, we have this unending aim of the world rulers of this darkness to circumvent the living, creative, and powerful Word of God. It is an ebb and flow throughout the years. The ebb is the work of darkness, and the flow is the work of the Lord Jesus by the Holy Spirit.

49

# The Battle of the Ages

We see it in the turning of the body of Christ into a religious organization. It is no longer a spiritual organism alive to its head, but an organization put together by man, based they say on the Word of God. Wherever we look in history, we see this onslaught on God's Word. We are informed by some Christians that it is not completely God's Word, but part of it is the work of human genius. That means you can take it or leave it as you please. According to these people, certain parts of it are the custom of the time and have no relevance for modern days, and therefore can be changed. Then, we have an assault that has wrecked the life of the Church. It began in Germany as a critical investigation as to whether the Bible is truly inspired by God. It spread all over the Christian world and destroyed the faith of many. It resulted in the dismemberment of Genesis, and the suggestion that the God of the Old Testament was a blood-thirsty deity who lived on the blood of the sacrifices of the worshipers. From this began the whole movement that the New Testament should be de-Judaized. In the modern era in which we live, this whole battle is reaching its crescendo. It has resulted in the Western nations turning away from the living God and turning back to the pagan days from which they originally came!

Similarly, there has been a continuous and violent assault on the Testimony of Jesus from the pouring out of the Spirit in Jerusalem at Pentecost until today. The early days of the Church were phenomenal. For the first time in the history of the universe, one hundred and twenty human beings, saved by the grace of God, were joined in a union with the Messiah enthroned at the right hand of God the Father. This union is described in the New Testament as head and body, a living organic union! It was destined to turn the Jewish world upside down and in the end also the Roman world. As long as the body of the Lord Jesus heard and obeyed its head, the Church was unstoppable. Satan's assault on the Testimony of Jesus was not only to destroy any faith in Him as the Word of God articulated, but to drive a wedge between Jesus as head and the body as the Church of God. This he did by reducing the spiritual and organic nature of the Church to a humanly led and energized organization. Of course, authority, eldership, and leadership are spiritual principles. The Word of God is clear: *Obey them that have the rule over you, and submit to them: for they watch in behalf of your souls, as they that shall give account; that they may do this with joy, and not with grief: for this were unprofitable for you* (Hebrews 13:17). The vital question is whether those leaders are born and developed by God and recognized by believers as such, or whether they are simply appointed by man. Every time the Church as the body of Christ has deteriorated and become something outward, organized, and humanly led, the Lord Jesus has taken the initiative and launched a new movement of the Spirit. It is as builder of the Church that the Lord Jesus has done this.

### WE NEED TO RESPOND

We need to respond to this. We are so used to merely drifting along complacently and not being disturbed or challenged. This is a divine challenge to become good and faithful soldiers of the Lord Jesus. The call of God is to war the good warfare! It is to **intercession that will entail our becoming a living sacrifice.** We are not ready for the discipline entailed in becoming good soldiers of the Lord Jesus, and normally we are not ready to function together as a unit. We have little sense of the togetherness that is strategically necessary to act as a unit. Obedience to the commander is vital in a military operation. Our commander is the Lord Jesus and in all intercession and prayer, we have to be obedient to His leading and prompting. When all the members of the unit are alive to His commands and leading, success is ensured.

The only answer to the situation which confronts us is to take refuge in the Lord; to be totally surrendered to His authority and will. Whatever it costs, we must be faithful to Him; we must not deny Him or the Truth He has given us. The apostle John on the Greek island of Patmos, detained in a Roman forced labor camp, wrote that he was there for the Word of God and for the Testimony of Jesus (Revelation 1:9). One would have thought that it was not an ideal condition in which to overcome, but by living faith, he did overcome. He was absolutely faithful to the Word of God and the Testimony of Jesus. As a result, the Lord gave Him revelation after revelation which was to become the completion of the sixty-six books and writings of the Bible. By his faithfulness to the Lord and by the Spirit of God and the Blood of the Lamb, he overcame. We must also by the grace of God and the power of the Holy Spirit do the same.

The prophet Joel not only described the condition which the people of God were facing, he also by the Spirit of God told them how to respond (see Joel 2:15-17). They were to blow the trumpet in Zion, sanctifying a fast, and calling a solemn assembly. There were no half measures in this! Everyone from the aged to the unweaned, from the newly married bridegroom to the bride, was to be in this together. The leaders were to intercede with passion, with genuine and great emotion. Their intercession was to come out of a burden conceived within them by the Holy Spirit. It was not just a matter of words but a deep pain within their hearts. Joel even outlined what should be their cry: *Spare Thy people and give not thy people to reproach, that the nations should rule over them.* (Joel 2:17). The Prophet saw clearly the goal of the forces of evil and darkness around Israel. Those forces would heathenize and paganize God's people, eclipsing the light of God shining in and through them. That was the supreme aim of Satan. He has always wanted to subjugate the redeemed to his will.

It is noteworthy that this is the same situation that we in the Western nations, once called Christian nations, are facing. We are watching a heathenizing and paganizing of our nations taking place at incredible speed. Shall we drift along with the current, believing that we can do nothing about this situation? Or shall we hear the cry of Joel from thousands of years ago? Shall we close our hearts to the call of the Spirit of God, or shall we open it to His burden?

# Chapter Four

## THE STRATEGIC NECESSITY OF INTERCESSION

In the first year of Darius the son of Ahasuerus, of the seed of the Medes, who was made king over the realm of the Chaldeans, in the first year of his reign I, Daniel, understood by the books the number of the years whereof the word of the Lord came to Jeremiah the prophet, for the accomplishing of the desolations of Jerusalem, even seventy years.

And I set my face unto the Lord God, to seek by prayer and supplications, with fasting and sackcloth and ashes. And I prayed unto the Lord my God, and made confession, and said, Oh, Lord, the great and dreadful God, who keepeth covenant and lovingkindness with them that love him and keep his commandments, we have sinned, and have dealt perversely, and have done wickedly, and have rebelled, even turning aside from thy precepts and from thine ordinances; neither have we hearkened unto thy servants the prophets, that spake in thy name to our kings, our princes, and our fathers, and to all the people of the land. O Lord, righteousness belongeth unto thee, but unto us confusion of face, as at this day; to the men of Judah, and to the inhabitants of Jerusalem, and unto all Israel, that are near, and that are far off, through all the countries whither thou hast driven them, because of their trespass that they have trespassed against thee. O Lord, to us belongeth confusion of face, to our kings, to our princes, and to our fathers, because we have sinned against thee. To the Lord our God belong mercies and forgiveness; for we have rebelled against him; neither have we obeyed the voice of the Lord our God, to walk in his laws, which he set before us by his servants the prophets. Yea, all Israel have transgressed thy law, even turning aside, that they should not obey thy voice: therefore hath the curse been poured out upon us, and the oath that is written in the law of Moses the servant of God; for we have sinned against him. And he hath confirmed his words, which he spake against us, and against our judges that judged us, by bringing upon us a great evil; for under the whole heaven hath not been done as hath been done upon Jerusalem. As it is written in the law of Moses, all this evil is come upon us: yet have we not entreated the favor of the Lord our God, that we should turn from our iniquities, and have discernment in thy truth. Therefore hath the Lord watched over the evil, and brought it upon us; for the Lord our God is righteous in all his works which he doeth, and we have not obeyed his voice. And now, O Lord our God, that hast brought thy people forth out of the land of Egypt with a mighty hand, and hast gotten thee renown, as at this day; we have sinned, we have done wickedly. O Lord, according to all thy righteousness, let thine anger and thy wrath, I pray thee, be turned away from thy city Jerusalem, thy holy mountain; because for our sins, and for the iniquities of our fathers, Jerusalem and thy people are become a reproach to all that are round about us. Now therefore, O our God, hearken unto the prayer of thy servant, and to his supplications, and cause thy face to shine upon thy sanctuary that is desolate, for the Lord's sake. O my God, incline thine ear, and hear; open thine eyes, and behold our desolations, and the city which is called by thy name: for we do not present our supplications before thee for our righteousness, but for thy great mercies' sake. O Lord, hear; O Lord, forgive; O Lord, hearken and do; defer not, for thine own sake, O my God, because thy city and thy people are called by thy name. (Daniel 9:1-19)

May we have a word of prayer:

*Beloved Lord, we want to thank You as we come to the ministry of Your Word, that You have provided for us an anointing. We recognize it, Lord. We can say a lot of words without the anointing and it will mean nothing. But Lord, we want to praise You that You have provided anointing both for the speaking of Your Word and the hearing of it. And into that anointing which You have provided for us by Your finished work on Calvary, we now stand by faith. Would You give a double portion of that anointing for this time. Challenge our hearts, instruct us and lead us in the way that we should go. And we ask it in the name of our Lord Jesus. Amen.*

### THE NEED FOR INTERCESSION

How are we to face this situation? There is, in fact, only one answer—intercession. Now the problem with intercession is that it is a word like being "born again," which is often bandied about amongst Christians and has little genuine meaning. We speak about born again people, this one is born again or that one. We speak about born again presidents or leaders, and very often they are not born again! The term intercession is often used, and it is not true intercession; it is prayer. There is a vast difference between prayer and intercession. Prayer is the pouring out of the heart. The apostle James states, "Ye have not because ye ask not" (James 4:2). That is prayer. We simply pour out our heart. We do not know what the will of the Lord is or even the way He wants to move in the situation which confronts us. However, we pour out our heart and plead with Him to hear us and to answer our prayer and longing that He will vindicate Himself, His Truth and His Name.

Intercession is in another dimension. It is the transmission by the Holy Spirit of the intercession and burden that is on the heart of the Lord Jesus. Intercession begins with **a knowledge of the will of God.** One must remember that Abraham could only intercede **when the Lord revealed to him** that he was going to judge Sodom and Gomorrah. Then Abraham began his intercession (see Genesis 18:20-33).

One must also remember how Moses reacted when the Lord said, "Stand aside, Moses, I am going to destroy this people. I am sick to death of their continual murmuring no matter what I do for them, whether in the way I lead them or the way I provide for them" (Exodus 32:7-14, author's paraphrase). He then said something, which I believe men in particular would find very appealing: "I will make of you a great nation." That should have struck a chord in Moses' heart. Instead, Moses reacted and began his intercession and said, "Lord, how can you do this? You have brought this people out of Egypt, and everybody knows You did it. You worked miracle after miracle, and by the blood of the lamb you brought them out of Egypt. And now you are going to destroy them? What will the nations say: 'He saved them to kill and destroy them?'" (Exodus 32:11-13, author's paraphrase). So began his intercession.

### DANIEL: THE GREAT INTERCESSOR

There are a number of great turning points in divine history as recorded in the Old Testament. Abraham was such a turning point as was Moses, Joshua, Samuel, David, Daniel, Nehemiah, and Ezra. Of them all, Daniel is probably the greatest example of an intercessor. All of these were intercessors used by God at these great turning points in divine history. The Lord has found and placed an intercessor at each of these points. To be an intercessor is the highest calling that any child of God could have. That calling surpasses the calling to be a prophet, or an apostle, or a teacher, or a shepherd or a pastor. It is the highest calling of God. It is as if God longs to bring His servants into **deep and powerful fellowship with Himself in the outworking and fulfillment of His will!**

For most Christians, Daniel is *the* prophet par excellence. He is the peak of prophecy. We have all kinds of matters and events that he foresaw, understood, and wrote down. However in our Jewish tradition, you will not find Daniel among the prophets; instead he is placed in the writings, the *K'tuvim.* The reason is that the Rabbis felt that to be an intercessor was a much higher and greater calling than to be a prophet. We placed at the beginning of this chapter the extraordinary paraphrase, or précis, of the intercessory ministry of Daniel. It all began in his quiet time. He was reading the scroll of the prophet Jeremiah and suddenly he came across this word:

"Seventy years are determined for the desolation of Jerusalem" (see Daniel 9:2). It was the impact of that word and the revelation of the Holy Spirit as to when the seventy years began, which catapulted Daniel into his ministry of intercession. It is worth noting that his ministry began with that discovery of the will of God. Whereas, so often with many believers, the discovery of God's will concerning any given situation is the conclusion of the matter: "If it is God's will it will happen anyway."

Now Daniel was the most important man next to the Sultan, the emperor. On his desk were all the various decrees that the emperor had made. They had to pass through his hands and then to the other leaders of the nation before finally becoming law. He was an incredibly busy man. Many people tell me that they are far too busy to be intercessors! However no one could be busier than Daniel was. His day began early and went on until late at night. His desk was filled with papers requiring him to read, study, pass on to others for their comment, and then to get them back to the emperor in order to obtain a final royal signature before becoming law. No man could have been busier than he, yet Daniel is *the* intercessor in the Old Covenant. Somewhere in the midst of his many onerous duties he found time to be an intercessor. Obviously, he had his spiritual priorities straight.

Businessmen sometimes tell me that they cannot possibly be intercessors because they have a business to run. Housewives sometimes tell me that they are far too busy with children in the home and demanding husbands to be intercessors. Everyone has an excuse for not being an intercessor! Daniel however is the best example we have of an intercessor. If it had not been for the intercessory ministry of Daniel, the Jewish people would never have returned to the land. They would never have rebuilt the temple, or rebuilt

Jerusalem and its walls, or rebuilt Bethlehem so that Micah's prophecy referring to Jesus could be fulfilled: *But thou, Bethlehem Ephrathah, which art little to be amongst the thousands of Judah, out of thee shall one come forth unto me that is to be the ruler in Israel* (5:2).

Consider moreover what Malachi said: *The Lord, whom you seek, will suddenly come to His temple* (3:1). There was no temple! It had been totally destroyed. It was the intercessory ministry of Daniel that brought about the return to the land and the rebuilding of the temple so that prophecy of Malachi could be fulfilled. There was no Nazareth, or Capernaum because they had been destroyed. There were many other cities I could mention which were also rebuilt with the return of the Jewish people.

When the people of God returned to the land, the most amazing fact about Daniel was that he did not return with them. He had lived for their return but he never went back. In the final analysis, his whole calling by God was centered in praying into fulfillment the purpose of God. To this day his grave is in Iran, or Persia. Why did he not go back? Typical of an intercessor, he had laid down his life; he had become a living sacrifice! To return to the land would have been for him the most pleasing and self-fulfilling, but he knew that there were enemies of the people of God in the high administration of the Persian Empire. He knew that he had to stay to his last breath in order to guard the return of the Jewish people for the rebuilding of the temple, the rebuilding of Jerusalem and its walls and the rebuilding of all the other cities. Therefore he stayed until he died.

### UNRESERVEDLY UNDER THE HEADSHIP OF THE LORD JESUS

The intercessory ministry of Daniel is incredible and has much to teach us about intercession. We will never be intercessors unless we surrender our entire will to the Lord. We have to be unreservedly under the government of God, ready to do whatever He tells us to do. In New Testament terms, it means we have to be under the headship of the Lord Jesus. What He burdens us with is where our intercession begins. What He reveals as His will is the grist for our intercession. Genuine intercession begins with the Lord Jesus and ends with the fulfillment of His will. He reveals His will for the situations we face. He is also the power to endure in our intercession.

## CORPORATE INTERCESSION

Intercession needs to be corporate. Now Daniel interceded alone; we do not hear of the three friends being with him. They were close friends who shared with him in everything, but whether they were with him in the intercession we do not know. We only have the paraphrase of his own ministry of intercession. However it is noteworthy that in the New Testament, intercession is very often corporate. When we are dealing with principalities, powers, world rulers of this darkness, and hosts of wicked spirits in the heavenlies, *we cannot deal with them alone.* When Paul writes about it, he writes, *we wrestle not against flesh and blood but against the principalities and powers.* It is a corporate thing. When you put on the armor, it is not only you personally; it is all of us together. Even more interesting is this question of the headship of Jesus. A good and valid time of intercession does not consist of potshots being fired here, there and everywhere—often at the enemy and occasionally at one another when we do not agree with the prayer or the theology within the offered prayer! Sometimes the infighting is very real!

I remember an occasion in the States in Hendersonville. I had been asked to lead a school of prayer there and people came from all over. It was a good time, but I have never forgotten one of the occasions when we were having practical times of intercession together. I warned them to stay away if they could not be corrected. But they all came and we had some marvelous times of intercession and prayer. I remember that they prayed for a certain backslidden brother whom I knew very well. Though they did not know him or anything about him, yet in intercession they actually came to the heart of that brother's problem. It was like an onion being peeled little by little, until they peeled all the layers and then finally they began to pray that the Lord would really deal with him.

Suddenly however after a little time of quiet, there was an old brother who cut across all the prayer and piped up and said: "We must pray for our sister Jessie in Florida." So I said to him, "What is wrong with our sister Jessie in Florida?" "Well," he said, "I had a phone call early this morning that she is desperately ill." Then I never heard anything like what followed. Someone got up immediately and said, "We pray for our sister. You have got to heal her because it is all in the Book! There is no such thing as ill health or disease. You must heal her! If you do not, that makes You a liar!" With that, others entered in and said, "Lord, we cannot possibly call You a liar! That is the most terrible thing!" Before long the whole group was firing at one another. It became the most wonderful theological discussion in the guise of prayer as to whether healing was an absolute must with no other option, or whether there were times when the will of God was to take somebody. It was dreadful. I just let them continue since they were so much enjoying killing one another and I thought it was best to let the matter take its course. However after about an hour I just said very weakly, "Lord bless this mess," and we all went to lunch.

At lunch there was a phone call from Florida. Our sister Jessie had gone to the Lord at 8:00 A.M. that morning. It was now 2:00 P.M. I could not wait for the reconvening of the meeting. As soon as they all came together I said, "It seems to me that you dear evangelicals are mostly Roman Catholics because you have spent a few hours this morning praying for the dead. Our sister is with the Lord and while you were all praying so frantically for her she was already with the Lord." From this we learned that sometimes sentiment can cut across the way the Lord is leading us in prayer.

Is it not incredible that when we have a group of people who are under the headship of Jesus, we discover that we are members of a body? He is the *Head* of the body. All its members are under the government and leadership of that Head. It is not you and the Lord alone; it is you and your fellow members. If we all are waiting for the word from the Lord, the Holy Spirit becomes the conductor. Everyone watches Him. Can you imagine a symphony in which someone with a cymbal just clanged it the whole time, or where violinists played just as they felt they should without any conductor? It would be a mess. However a real time of corporate intercession is something marvelous because it is the reality of what we believe. The Head, who is at the right hand of God by the Holy Spirit, is leading and harmonizing everybody together. So the vital and strategic matter in corporate intercession is the headship of Jesus by the Holy Spirit.

### INTERCESSION BEGINS WITH A KNOWLEDGE OF THE WILL OF GOD

Intercession begins with a knowledge of the will of God. Once we know what the will of God is, then intercession begins because we can stand together with the Lord for the fulfillment of His will. It is not hit and miss because we know what His will is. As we have already previously mentioned, we have it in the pattern prayer of the Lord (Matthew 6:9-13). The Lord Jesus taught us to pray, *Thy kingdom come. Thy will be done **as in heaven, so on earth*** (note the original Greek). In other words, *we have to know what the will of heaven is.* Once we have an understanding of what the will of God is in any given situation which we are facing, we can by the power of the Holy Spirit stand for its enforcement. Thus we pray for example, "Lord, let Your kingdom come into this situation. Let Your throne rule in this situation. Let Your will be done as in heaven so on earth in this matter." In other words, intercession is the *enforcing* of the will of God when everything seems against it. This is a very important lesson to learn, especially with regard to Daniel.

### DANIEL DISCOVERED THE WILL OF GOD

Through the Holy Spirit, Daniel had discovered in reading the prophecy of Jeremiah that seventy years were determined for the desolation of Jerusalem. The extraordinary fact is that he not only discovered that seventy years were determined, but the Holy Spirit revealed to him when those seventy years began! Many Bible teachers believe it began with King Zedekiah, who was the last of the kings of Judah, however it was not him; it was King Jehoiachin. Only the Spirit of God could have so led Daniel to discover this and by that leading discover the will of God for the Jewish people in exile.

Daniel had an imperial mind because he was part of a huge empire and understood all the inner workings of empire politics. Very quickly he made the calculations: "Good gracious! We have only two years to go! We are nearly there! The seventy years are nearly exhausted." Now, if he had been like many Charismatics, he would have said to Shadrach, Meshach and Abednego, "Come on boys, let's have a ball! We will have a marvelous time of praise together. We will just worship the Lord because He is going to do it!" Instead, Daniel threw ashes on his head, clothed himself in sackcloth, and began to fast. You might think, "What has he read in Jeremiah which brought him to such a conclusion?" **It is just here that we find that Daniel is a *real* intercessor.** He had discovered what the will of God was and by the Holy Spirit discovered when the seventy years began and therefore when it was going to end. *Thus he got to work and entered his powerful ministry of intercession*!

We have an incredible précis of this ministry in Daniel 9:1-19. It is almost as if he had no faith. "Lord," he said, "forgive this people. See what they have done?" He did not even say, "they-they-they." He said, "*We* have dealt perversely; *we* have sinned against You. To *us* belongs confusion of face." You might feel you want to lay hold of him and say, "Daniel! You are the one who would not eat the king's dainties. You believed so much in the kashrut law (kosher law); you would not even defile yourself with some of those foods. You could have lost your life because you were so faithful to the Lord and to the precepts of the Law of Moses. How can you include yourself in the sin and iniquities of Israel? Of all the people in the exile, you seemed to stand alone for you never compromised."

## WALKING WITH AND HEARING THE LORD

Daniel, however, understood something about intercession: when the Lord reveals His will and His purpose, **we have to pray it into being.** Then we understand the meaning of "Your kingdom come, your will be done, as in heaven, so on earth." If we are not walking with the Lord, if we are not hearing the Lord, we have a problem. Jesus said, "My sheep hear my voice" (John10:27). I know a lot of people, especially fellows, who say, "The Lord would never talk to me. He speaks to sisters but I do not think He speaks to men." The fact of the matter is you can stop the Lord's speaking to you because you do not believe He ever will!

There was a sister who was a burden to us at Halford House. She was not part of the fellowship but lived about sixty to eighty miles away. She was always trying to get through to me on the phone. So the whole staff at Halford would save me from her by either trying to talk to her or by trying to fob her off in one way or another. She was an absolute menace! She used to get through late in the evening when I was still studying for the Bible study. I was the only person in the place and I would take up the phone and she would then *burst* out saying, "Oh! Praise the Lord! I prayed that I would get through to you. The Lord has given you such wisdom. The Lord has blessed you with the spirit of counsel and wisdom and I need it." Then she would pour out her problem. I could not get a word in edgeways. You could not say, "Sister! Shut up for a moment." You could not say one thing to her. She *poured* out whatever her problem was like a great torrent. Then suddenly without even breathing she would say, "Thank you dear Lance, for counseling me in this way. You have counseled me with such wisdom. God has given you incredible wisdom. Thank you!" With that she put the phone down before I had a chance to say anything! After a time whenever she would phone, I would just say, "Yes, yes," and put the phone down and carry on with my Bible study. Then I would take it up again and say, "Yes, yes," and put it down and carry on. It was such a waste of time. She did not want me to say anything; she was deluded. She actually believed I was counseling her, but I never got a word in edgeways.

That is like so many Christians. They say to the Lord, "Lord, you are full of wisdom and knowledge. All the treasures of wisdom and knowledge are hidden in You. The Spirit of counsel is in You; You are the Wonderful Counselor!

I worship at Your footstool," and they never give Him a chance to say anything! So it is as if they put the phone down and say, "I have had a wonderful time with the Lord." Yet He has never been able to say anything! Some people would drop dead if the Lord said, "Shut up, I have something to say to you!" I think about this in some of our prayer meetings. We never expect the Lord to speak to us. The Lord, however, *can* speak to us, sometimes through someone who reads to us a Scripture laid on his or her heart during the prayer time, which can be prophetic. When they give it, it is like a sudden shaft of light, which comes into the whole intercession. Sometimes, this can come through in the use of a prophetic gift.

### GENUINE INTERCESSION IS SPIRITUALLY STRATEGIC

Daniel lived to see the children of God go back to the land. So vital was Daniel's intercessory ministry that the Archangel Gabriel was expressly sent to him to give to him that "mathematical prophecy" concerning the coming of the Messiah Jesus. Everything in Daniel's life and calling to be an intercessor then fell into place. That prophecy was given to him by God, whilst he was still in the middle of the battle of intercession (see Daniel 9:20-27). **That must have transformed Daniel's intercession** because he suddenly realized, "All that I have suffered, the position that God has given me in the Persian Empire next to the Sultan, is not by accident. It is by the foreordination of the Lord. It is related to the coming of the Messiah. The Promised Land has to be recovered; the temple has to be rebuilt; the city of Jerusalem and these other cities and towns have to be rebuilt so that certain prophecies can be fulfilled, and gloriously the Messiah can come on time." It must have **transformed** him!

Daniel certainly had deeply suffered from the Babylonians; many of his close relatives had been murdered by them. He had forcibly been enlisted into Imperial service

67

which meant that his masculinity had been taken from him. One could not be part of the Imperial service without being made a eunuch. All of this could have made him an in-turned and incredibly bitter person. Instead, he realized it was God's preparation of him to be part of the fulfillment not of Persian history but of Divine history. He stands at one of the greatest turning points in divine history as one that prayed into being the purpose and will of God. Is it going too far to write that there would have been no restoration of the land of Israel, no Bethlehem, no Jerusalem, no Nazareth, and no glorious birth of the Messiah, if Daniel had not surrendered himself to the Lord? Daniel became a living sacrifice and turned his sufferings into glory.

We have entitled this chapter "The Strategic Necessity of Intercession." Certainly Daniel's intercession was **strategic**! The forces of darkness and evil furiously fought against Daniel's intercession and testimony. They did everything they could to destroy him. Through his intercession the purpose of God for world redemption by the birth, death, resurrection, and ascension of the Messiah Jesus was fulfilled. For this reason, God sent the Archangel Gabriel to Daniel to strengthen him in that intercessory ministry and to make him realize that it was not even and only the *physical* restoration of Israel, but it was supremely related to the coming of the Messiah, to His work of universal redemption.

From this we learn one of the greatest lessons about intercession. If it is true that we are praying into realization and fulfillment the will of God in any given world situation, **it is related to the final coming of the Messiah**! God could do all that is required by Himself without us. Indeed it might be much easier for Him to do it alone. The incredible fact is that He chooses to work and act with those who are prepared to be intercessors at whatever the cost entailed. In intercession, He shares with us His will and purpose, and then through our intercessory prayer acts on it. It is divine fellowship in action! It is as if God refuses to act without the human fellowship with Him of those whom He redeems (see Ezekiel 22:30).

# Chapter Five

## I SOUGHT FOR A MAN TO STAND IN THE GAP

> And I sought for a man among them, that should build up the wall, and stand in the gap before me for the land, that I should not destroy it; but I found none. Therefore have I poured out mine indignation upon them; I have consumed them with the fire of my wrath: their own way have I brought upon their heads, saith the Lord God. (Ezekiel 22:30-31)

### BUT I FOUND NONE

These words recorded by the Prophet Ezekiel, expressed the heart cry of God to find at least one person in Israel that would stand in the gap before Him in intercession. It reveals that even when terrible and consuming judgment is predicted, the tenderness and the love of God longs to find a means to ameliorate the judgment. The four words "but I found none" express the divine sorrow. It is incredible that not one soul in all the thousands of Israel was ready to stand in the gap. We believers in the last stages of world history are facing a similar situation. May it never be true of our generation that the Lord would say "But I found none."

### THE POSSIBILITY OF A SPIRITUAL AWAKENING

As we consider the situation in the Western nations, all the once called Christian nations, we find that the greatest need at this present time is genuine intercession. There is nothing that could save the United States, Canada, or the Western nations other than a huge spiritual awakening. God has done it before and He can do it again! However, is it His will? Once we have discovered His will in this situation, our intercession can begin. No matter how impossible the problems confronting us may seem to be, with God nothing is impossible. These nations could become the scene of one of the greatest awakenings and revivals in the history of the Church. In the midst of enormous pressures, breakdowns in government, corruption in high places, the collapse of morality and ethical standards, and the ongoing paganization of these nations, God could still do something in and through His redeemed people and save multitudes of the unsaved.

I have described the persistent and continuous encroachment of darkness and evil upon the national society of these once so called Christian nations. Nevertheless the Lord can overcome this problem and by the Holy Spirit sweep thousands into His kingdom. The question is simple and stark: who is prepared to pay the price? Everyone talks about past awakenings and revivals, but are we prepared to pay the price! If the Lord would touch our present dark and evil situation, there will have to be some believers who will meet together in sacrificial fellowship and give themselves to continuous and enduring intercession until He breaks into it. Matthew Henry once wrote: "Whenever God is going to do something, He first sets His people to prayer." Where are the believers who are ready for such a commitment?

## GOD DESIRES FELLOWSHIP

Those who have read what I have written so far may wonder why God needs our intercession for the fulfillment of *His* will! Surely, it would be better if He worked alone to bring it to pass. Knowing the Lord's people as I do, I think it would be much better if the Lord simply said, "I will do it Myself." Normally we are a load of trouble one way or another; even the best of us gets in the way. However, God believes in fellowship. Almost the first word in the Bible is: "Let Us make man in Our image" (Genesis 1:26). He says: "Us." There is a fellowship even within the Godhead. The whole meaning of the Lord Jesus being the Head and we being the body is fellowship. The body is not one member; it is many members, but only one body. That one body has only one Head; it is the Lord Jesus. It is almost as if the Lord is saying: "I want to do so much in these nations, but I will not unless some of you are prepared to pay the price. Then in fellowship with Me, we will do it together."

Some of those who are reading this book might wonder if I am not putting the whole responsibility for awakenings on the redeemed people of God. On this matter it is necessary to be absolutely clear and forthright. Awakenings, revivals, and renewals are all sovereign acts of God Himself. Awakenings are times when suddenly everyone becomes conscious of the holiness of God, of the presence of God, and of our sin and short comings. All of these are powerful initiatives of the Lord Jesus as the builder of the true Church. He launches them again and again when the Church is in danger of being derailed or misled. Nevertheless, the Almighty and Sovereign God *desires fellowship* with those whom He saves. We are *co-workers* together with Him. It is not our will that is being fulfilled but His will. The Lord Jesus said, *Take my yoke upon you and learn of me; for I am meek and lowly in heart: and ye shall find rest unto your souls. For my yoke is easy, and my burden is light* (Matthew 11:29-30).

The Lord Jesus was talking of the double yoke which was used in oxen or horses employed for plowing and doing other heavy agricultural work. It is astounding that the Lord Jesus who could do the whole work and bear the burden alone and very well, longs that we should be yoked with Him in the fulfillment of His will.

## IN INTERCESSORY MINISTRY GOD IS TRAINING US

The reason the Lord gives such importance to genuine intercession is that through it He teaches us how to discern His mind and discover His will, and then by his grace and power to stand with him and pray it into being. It is actually learning to reign with Christ. Long before we are the bride who will reign with Him forever, we are being taught how to reign with Him now. Many of us believers know nothing about reigning. We cannot even reign over the pet dog, let alone the kitchen sink, the home, the family, or the business. Sometimes believers ask me, "Is it true that we are going to reign over areas of the earth with the Lord?" If they carry the same mess in their home, their business, and in the church to the areas over which they will reign, the Lord save us from it! Within the battle of intercession, God teaches us how to reign over quite small matters, then larger matters, then finally brings us to the place where we can reign with Him in eternity. When we have learnt how by the Spirit of the Lord to discern His mind, to distinguish it from other ideas, and to stand for the fulfillment of His will, however long it takes, we learn one of the greatest lessons we can learn. It will stand us in good stead in every other aspect of our lives.

### FOR OUR ENCOURAGEMENT

Let me encourage you to believe that nothing is impossible with God. First we have to discover what His will is, whether in small matters related to our homes and families or local fellowships, or large matters relating to super powers or worldwide situations. Then in fellowship with one another under the leadership of the Lord Jesus, we have to learn how to endure and persist in our intercession until His will is realized. Let me give a few examples.

### *The Soviet Union and Its Satellites*

From time to time in Halford House we had prayer and Bible weeks. Dennis Clark of blessed memory and Alec Buchanan also of blessed memory, who are both now with the Lord, used to come and lead times of prayer, meditation and intercession. On one occasion, which I shall never forget, they said to me, "Do you not think we should pray for Russia? It is like a vast prison and has shed so much innocent blood. Should we not pray for them to be free?" So we brought it to the whole fellowship and I wondered, "Will the fellowship be able to rise to this?" After all, many Christians thought Marxism was *the* antichrist. They would say, "There is no way that you are going to overcome it; it is going to take the whole world." However, we brought it to the fellowship and we had the most incredible morning and afternoon sessions, praying that Russia would be free and that believers would be able to take the gospel to the ends of the Soviet Union and wherever she had influence over other nations, in Eastern Europe, in the Balticum, and in Central Asia. In many ways the Soviet Union was the largest single problem to the Free World, apart from being one large prison camp. It believed in the export of its Marxist doctrine to the rest of the world, and the enslavement of the world by violence, blood, and war.

In the third session in the evening the sense of the Lord's presence was marvelous. Dennis quietly walked across from where he was seated to where I was seated and whispered in my ear, "Do you think tonight, we could break the power of the Soviet Union?" And I said, "What do you mean?" He said, "That it be free." "Free?" I said. "Yes, free," he said. "Well," I said, "that would be incredible." So he turned around and went back and I saw him whispering in Alec's ear. Then the two of them came across and said, "We believe in this session, we have come to a point of faith where we can take action in the Name of the Lord." They continued, "We believe as leader of the fellowship here, you ought to lead in this." So I found myself, as it were, suddenly thrown to the lions. Then I broke in and said to everybody, "Our brothers feel, we all feel, that we should continue further in this. We need now to take action in the Name of the Lord. We have been given the keys of the kingdom to actually see to it that what heaven wills shall be fulfilled." Many believers have misunderstood that word about the keys being given to Peter. The Lord Jesus said:

> I will give unto thee [to Peter, which is to the Church] the keys of the kingdom of heaven: and whatsoever thou shalt bind on earth shall be bound in heaven; and whatsoever thou shalt loose on earth shall be loosed in heaven. (Matthew 16:19)

However, in the Greek the verbal tense is better translated: *Whatsoever you bind on earth, shall have been bound in heaven, and whatsoever you loose on earth, shall have been loosed in heaven.* In other words, you can only enforce what is the will of heaven!

Then I said to everyone, "Shall we take action for this in the Name of the Lord?" That time of prayer turned into the most glorious time of worship and praise. No one who was there will ever forget it. It went on until midnight, just worshipping and praising the Lord. Finally when we closed down the session, I said to everyone, "More surely than I stand here this evening, the Soviet Union will be free." It took a little while and then it happened! It began with Poland and Lech Walesa, and Poland became free! Then it started in Hungary and spread to Bulgaria and Czechoslovakia. All of a sudden the Iron Curtain disappeared like mist before the rising sun. We had lived our lives within the shadow of the Iron Curtain ever since the end of the Second World War, and it just disappeared. Then in Germany, the Berlin wall which divided the city was hacked down by the people, and East and West Germany became one for the first time in many decades. It was incredible.

Far more remarkable was the fact that the blood-red flag with the old hammer and sickle of the Soviet Union disappeared, and in its place the old Czarist flag with its red, white and blue was restored. Even more remarkable was the return of the emblem of the double headed eagle with the crown between its two heads. The next time you see Vladimir Putin addressing his cabinet look above his head and you will see it on the wall. No one could have believed such a thing was possible. No one! To believe that the old flag would come back and then that the double headed eagle of the Romanovs with the crown between the two heads should once again be above the Russian cabinet is incredible.

The last event was even more amazing. A service of repentance was held. Boris Yeltsin was President of Russia at that time, and he was present with other leaders of the government and the Patriarchs of the Russian church. They had candles, vestments, and pictures of the Czar, Czarina and the Czarivic and they all walked round the Kremlin wall repenting for their murder. Could anyone have believed that such an event could ever have taken place?

From that point the gospel has gone all over Russia, Hungary, Romania, Bulgaria, Czechoslovakia, Poland, and many other places such as Uzbekistan, Kirgizstan, and Kazakhstan. When I spoke at the Convocation of the Nations in Jerusalem, I remember being so amazed when certain brothers tried to put a robe on me. They were Kazaks from Kazakhstan, and they said, "We want to make you a patriarch of the Kazaks." I said, "Well, that is very sweet of you but I do not know what the point of my becoming a patriarch would be." Nevertheless, they draped me in a marvelous blue robe and then this brother said to me, "You see these six men? Every one of them is a pastor. They are all Muslims who have found the Lord in the last few years and every one of them is the leader of an assembly that consists of not less than one thousand."

# The Battle of the Ages

Do you believe that in a prayer meeting a spiritual battle could be fought and won and something as impossible as the breakup of the Soviet Union could result? If it is possible with the Soviet Union, with all its years of wickedness, could it not happen elsewhere in other impossible situations? I should also mention that the Marxist Manifesto, which was signed in the Kremlin palace seventy years before to the day, was annulled seventy years later in the same Kremlin. Seventy in Scripture has great significance. Seven in Hebrew thought is the figure which denotes fullness or completeness. Seventy means a complete period of time. Is that not amazing? What I have recorded here does not mean that Russia will not play some dark and evil part in the last events of world history as we know it (see Ezekiel 38-39). It does mean that through intercession national matters can be changed and large numbers of people can come into a saving experience of the Lord!

I could tell many more stories but the fact of the matter is that nothing is impossible with God. Is it possible to bring back our national constitutions, as they were originally? Do we believe that those freedoms which we are in danger of losing, for which some gave their blood, could be reinforced? Or should we throw in our glove and say, "Well, it is part of the days of evil that we are living in"? The necessity is to find out what the will of God is. Then we shall have all the weapons we need. It is when we are together, enabled by the Spirit of God to pronounce and declare the will of God, that it will happen. I could give many examples of other national matters and events that at different times we have been involved in, and seen the Lord triumph. My point in telling this story is that nothing is impossible with God. Once we have discovered the will of God, no matter how huge the matter is, how worldwide it is, or how entrenched it is, with God it is possible!

## CONTINUE ON IN INTERCESSION UNTIL THE LORD ANSWERS

In many ways, the whole assembly and work of the Lord centered in Halford House in Richmond, England was a result of the Hebrides Revival. I am recounting the story for the encouragement of all who are reading this book. The story of the Hebrides Revival and the story of Halford House is a vast encouragement to continue and to endure in prayer warfare through the battle until He fulfills His will. Once that will of the Lord is clearly understood by those who are giving themselves to intercession, the battle begins.

### *The Hebrides Revival in Scotland*

When the Hebrides revival hit the northwest isles of Scotland in the beginning of the 1950s, it began with two old sisters, Peggy and Christine Smith, one was eighty-four and the other eighty-two. One of them was blind and the other was crippled with arthritis. They persisted in prayer for revival for the Hebrides islands. They were deeply burdened by the state of the Church, especially in their own parish. No young people ever attended any of the meetings. They became so painfully burdened that they began to set aside two days a week to seek the Lord in prayer concerning the Spiritual situation. On one of those two days they would start prayer at 10:00 in the evening and they remained on their knees until 3:00 or 4:00 in the morning.

Peggy Smith had a dream in which she understood that revival was coming. As the two sisters persisted in intercession, the Spirit of the Lord created in them an unshakable conviction that revival was near. The Lord had given them a specific promise:

# The Battle of the Ages

> For I will pour water upon him that is thirsty, and streams upon the dry ground; I will pour my Spirit upon thy seed, and my blessing upon thine offspring: and they shall spring up among the grass, as willows by the watercourses (Isaiah 44:3-4).

They had understood that the Lord was speaking about young people coming into the salvation of God. They took hold of that promise day after day for some years until finally it happened. At the same time, there was a group of men who met together regularly in a barn for intercession. They also had a spiritual promise given to them by God and would not let it go until He fulfilled it.

The two deeply burdened sisters had spoken to the minister of their church, asking him if he would not call the church office bearers to prayer, to the same persistent intercession. The minister, who had a deep regard for the sisters, called on the church officers to intercede in the same manner. Seven brothers responded and also received a promise that the Lord would pour out His Spirit on the Hebrides. They met together twice weekly in that barn in persistent prayer.

One of the sisters had a vision in which she saw her parish church crowded to the doors with young people and a minister standing in the pulpit that she did not recognize. That vision was fulfilled when a good and faithful brother from Edinburgh, Duncan Campbell, came to the Hebrides. He always said that he was not responsible for the revival, but that it was the Holy Spirit who was responsible. However, the Holy Spirit used Duncan Campbell mightily. It was amazing what began to happen simultaneously all over the island. In many cases, meetings in church buildings that were not advertised were filled with people who had just come together. It was truly the work of the Holy Spirit. People fell down on their faces crying out to be delivered from their sin and evil. In the years which followed 1949, it happened all over the islands. In many cases, men and women would fall on their faces in the wet heather and lie there for an hour or two. So powerful was the outpouring of the Spirit that fishermen were saved while they were on their trawlers. They fell on their faces while bringing in the nets and called upon God for mercy, and they came back not only with the fish but saved by the grace of God. Shepherds on the hills with their sheep fell on their faces on the wet grass and called upon God to save them and forgive them their sins. Like all true awakenings of the Holy Spirit, it was an all-consuming consciousness of the Presence of a Holy God. Thousands came to a saving knowledge of the Lord Jesus. It was the Hebrides revival!

Only such an outpouring of the Spirit of God can save the U.S. and the Western Nations. Charles Finney said you can always have an awakening if you are prepared to pay the price and sacrifice yourself. May God speak to us.

### Prayer and Awakening in the Thames Valley

In Richmond upon Thames, we had four months of prayer every night and out of that came the fellowship at Halford House. It was a God given burden that resulted in continuous and enduring intercession. It was the story of the Hebrides Revival that first sparked the burden. That God given burden was so heavy and painful that we interceded for relief! After each evening of prayer we felt the burden lifted, only to discover that the burden was still there the next morning, as strong as ever.

There were eight of us who originally shared the same burden and in each session of those four months we were never more than eight and never less than two or three. During those times we endured the two worst smogs of London's history, each one of them lasting at least six to seven days. During those times all transport ceased and the hospitals were filled with those who had lung problems. On each occasion, at least three thousand people died. Although to reach the prayer session, we had to walk three to five miles in the smog, not one of those prayer times was canceled. We had no idea that the fellowship at Halford was the answer to our prayers. We even wondered if it was the enemy taking us away from that for which we were praying, which was revival, renewal and awakening in the Thames valley.

Later we had four years of prayer at Halford House. No one noticed at the time that the four years began on the same date that we had begun the four months of prayer. Instead of months it was years. We were burdened that the Lord would do something new in the Church worldwide. That He would pour out His Spirit everywhere and bring us into a new understanding of His purpose and a new deeper experience of Himself. We prayed every night for three years and then suddenly in the most incredible time of prayer the Lord broke in. That time of prayer seemed rather listless and lifeless at its beginnings and I remember thinking to myself, "Are we not *flogging a dead horse*? I must speak with one of the elders as to whether we should stop these times of prayer." It was that night that the Lord broke in, and it was as if we were looking into heaven. Someone said, "The walls have come down," and that is exactly how we all felt. We decided, "We cannot go on praying because the Lord has clearly spoken." So we said, "What can we do?" Then we said, "We will have a time of worship every night; in which we shall thank the Lord for what He is going to do."

It was during those times of that fourth year, that we first heard of a whole company of believers in the west of Wales who had been meeting in their normal routine, and the Holy Spirit fell on them, knocking them all over the place and doing something extraordinary. Then we heard that in an old Methodist chapel which was lifeless in the West Country, the

Holy Spirit had fallen on them on a Sunday morning. They spoke in tongues, which horrified us to begin with. "They spoke in tongues?!?!" Then we heard of something in the North of England. Before long, we saw it everywhere on all sides. The most amazing report was a place in Putney, a part of London like a rabbit warren, where the Lord fell on what had been a dead company. The poor pastor was out with his dog and suddenly felt weak around the knees. He saw a bench, went and sat on it, threw back his head and spoke in a tongue. He had never done anything like that before! He could not believe what had happened to him. His dog sat there looking at him as if wondering, "What has happened to him?" Then he returned home only to find that his wife had exactly the same experience at the same moment in the kitchen. It transformed that fellowship. For the first time in forty years they had conversions, baptisms, healings, and all kinds of miracles. It then began to happen everywhere. All of this and much more was the beginning of the Charismatic revival through which millions worldwide would come into a saving knowledge of the Lord Jesus.

I shall never forget when someone rang the door and there was a missionary from Nepal. I had known her from when I was a boy. She had always been like an older sister to me. I took one look at her and she was radiant. I thought, "It is not the same person." Then she said, "Have you time for a spot of fellowship?" She had never before asked *me* for a spot of fellowship. She was always there ready to tell me what to do or what not to do. I said to her, "Have you had an experience of the Holy Spirit?" She responded, "How could you tell?" It happened everywhere, all over the place. I know that there were others who were praying as well as us, but we felt so amazed that the Lord had used us for four years of nightly prayer until it happened.

## *The Welsh Revival*

The Welsh Revival had its beginnings in 1903, and progressed in power through 1904 and onwards. It was one of the most powerful awakenings to hit the British Isles. Hundreds of thousands were swept into the kingdom of God and Welsh life was characterized by it. Nearly every denomination during its course was revived and was brought back to the biblical principles of their beginnings. Similarly, every missionary organization received a new input of power and life. It touched every part of the United Kingdom: Wales, Ireland, Scotland, and England. Indeed in one way or another, it touched the whole world.

It seems the first signs of a coming awakening and revival were in 1903, principally in a burden of prayer in many individuals. By 1904 to 1905 it became a huge river of salvation and transformation. Evan Roberts, at 26 years of age, was the generally acclaimed leader. Although He was a man of the Word of God, and a man of prayer, he himself always said he was not the leader of the awakening but that it was led by the Holy Spirit. He would often awaken at 1:00 A.M. and pray until 5:00 A.M. Sometimes he prayed so loudly that his landlady in the end asked him to leave the accommodation. At the same time, there were also other believers upon whom the Holy Spirit fell in power in many parts of Wales, who similarly had the same enormous burden of prayer for an awakening. That burden in them became a travail of spirit until the awakening and revival became a reality.

Within six months, at least 100,000 people had been converted. Drunkenness dropped, public houses and bars were empty, as also were brothels and gambling dens. Pit donkeys in the coal mines, accustomed to kicks and obscenities to get them to move and to work, stopped working because so many of the coal miners were saved and transformed. I once asked two very old ladies who witnessed the whole awakening what their greatest memory of it was. They said apart from the amazing conversion of hardened and coarse sinners, it was the singing that came from underneath the ground all over the town. It was the saved coal miners at work in the mines, worshiping the Lord with singing.

This awakening touched every aspect of Welsh life and character. It affected, as I have said, not only Wales but Ireland, Scotland and England. Within years it was to touch and affect all parts of the world. David Lloyd George, who was himself Welsh and who became Prime Minister of Great Britain, at the time of the First World War (1914-18) and the Balfour declaration (1917), said "It seems to be rocking Welsh life like a great earthquake." Certainly, it characterized Welsh life right through both the First and Second World Wars. When I was doing my national service in the 1950's in the Royal Air Force in Egypt, I noticed as a believer that even the Welsh rugby players had spiritual character which distinguished them from the other rugby players.

### *The Moravians*

I have mentioned the Hebrides Revival, the Charismatic Revival, and the Welsh Revival, but these are three awakenings out of many others which I could have also mentioned. The Moravian Revival led by Nicholas Count Zinzendorf was an incredible awakening with an enormous influence upon worldwide missions. Count Zinzendorf loved the Lord Jesus passionately from an early age. It seems that the Lord's hand was on him from his beginnings. It was however when he stood transfixed before an oil painting of the crucified Messiah with the words in German underneath, "I have done all this for you, what have you done for Me?" that something happened! He had been long converted, but he had stood immobilized before that painting with the challenge of total surrender to the Lord Jesus. He accepted the challenge and surrendered his all to the Lord. It was the beginning of one of the most remarkable moves of the Holy Spirit in the history of the Church. It led to the hundred year continuous prayer meeting, and missionaries by choice going to the most inaccessible areas of the world. For example, they went to the Arctic, to the Eskimos; to the basically ignored and overlooked lepers; to the slaves being shipped to the New World; to the highest point in the world, Tibet. By the Holy Spirit, that total surrender of his being to the Lord was reproduced in thousands of others. They too became living sacrifices, and the world was never the same. It is the same spiritual character which led C.T. Studd to found one of the largest missionary organizations in the history of missions. That same character found in Nicolas Count Zinzendorf and C.T. Studd is summed up in C.T.'s words: "If Jesus Christ be God and died for me, then no sacrifice can be too great for me to make for Him."

Spiritually, the Moravians were the result of the Holy Spirit powerfully moving through Jan Huss and Comenius. Jan Huss and John Wycliffe have often been called the morning star of the Reformation. That move brought hundreds of thousands to a saving knowledge of the Lord Jesus in central Europe. Those people were called by Roman Catholics Hussites and violently persecuted. In fact Jan Huss through the deceit of the Catholic Church was given a safe passage to come to Konstanz to a conference with the Catholic leaders. When he arrived he was arrested and immediately condemned as a heretic and burnt at the stake. The Hussites and the Bohemian Brethren were driven out of most places in which they had lived and worked, and their persecution reached new heights of savagery and brutality.

Nicolas Count Zinzendorf opened his estate bordering on Bohemia and Moravia to all these persecuted believers, and thousands took refuge in it. These Hussites and Bohemian Brethren came to be known as the Moravians. As one would expect, with all the differences of background, of traditions, and of spiritual outlook, there were large problems, heated discussion, and little unity. As a result of Count Zinzendorf's plea for unity and the impassioned prayer of some believers for unity, there were a number of occasions when the Holy Spirit moved upon them all. It culminated on the thirteenth day of August 1727 when the Holy Spirit was poured out on the whole assembly and loud weeping drowned out the singing during worship at the Lord's Table. The Holy Spirit baptized the whole fellowship. The result was that all the differences were melted into unity. The hundred year non-stop prayer meeting was born in that same summer.

Within a year (1728), they held their first missionary meeting. It was to result finally in 300 missionaries being sent out in 65 years and the founding of 226 Moravian mission stations, before William Carey (often called the father of modern missions) was even born!

## *The First Great Evangelical Awakening*

The First Great Evangelical Awakening in the eighteenth century was destined not only to bring millions of unsaved people to the Lord but was to affect and transform nations. For this reason, it is called the *Great* Evangelical Awakening. It was to deeply affect the worldwide empire of Great Britain and also all of North America.

The three main leaders of this enormous awakening which began early in the eighteenth century in Britain, are by general acclaim John Wesley, his brother Charles Wesley, and George Whitefield. Turned out of church after church as a result of their preaching, they began to preach in the open air to tens of thousands of people. George Whitefield was the first to preach in the open air.

John and Charles Wesley were both born into a family devoted to the Lord Jesus. Their parents were godly, and they grew up religious but not saved. At that point, their Christianity was outward and ritualistic. Their mother, Susanna Wesley, bore nineteen children, of whom only three survived to maturity. There is no doubt that her effect on both John and Charles was character forming. Their father was a vicar in the Church of England. Both John and Charles grew to maturity without a saving experience of the Lord Jesus. Nevertheless, at Oxford they formed the "Holy Club" to help the members of it to be pious and holy.

George Whitefield's experience was quite different. He was born in Gloucester and grew up in a tavern, no stranger to alcoholics and to the world in general. Whilst at Oxford, George Whitefield joined the Holy Club and became lifelong friends with John and Charles, in spite of some deep differences in doctrine. John and Charles were whole-hearted Arminians and George was a whole-hearted Calvinist. George was the first in the group to experience an inward spiritual transformation by the Holy Spirit. He was born again, and from that point he was the first of the three to preach the necessity of a new birth!

Having been ordained at Oxford, John Wesley accepted a call to be a minister to British Colonists in Savannah, Georgia. He joined a ship sailing to the New World. On board was a group of forty Moravian missionaries, who were going to the New World to reach the Red Indians. Somewhere in the mid-Atlantic, the ship hit a huge storm. The captain and the sailors began to lighten the vessel but felt there was very little hope of survival. John became suddenly aware that there was a real possibility of meeting God and began to panic. Suddenly, he heard in the bowels of the ship the sound of hymn singing and he wondered if the ship had already gone down, and that he was on the other side unsaved! As he wondered, he saw a door slightly ajar and light coming out from it. He made for the door and quietly pushed it open. To his surprise, he saw forty Moravians singing with joy and calmness, with babies in their arms and toddlers on their knees. It was at that point that he realized they were not afraid of dying. They had a faith and an experience of the Lord which he did not possess. This feeling never left him in the two years that he was a missionary in the Colonies, seeking to convert the Red Indians. In the end, he returned to Britain a failed missionary. He wrote in his journal: "I went to America to convert the Indians; but O! Who shall convert me?" Back in Britain, he heard that there was a meeting in Aldersgate Street, in the city of London. In that meeting, someone was going to read Luther's preface to Romans. John Wesley went to that meeting and whilst Luther's preface to the Roman letter was being read he felt, "my heart was strangely warmed." It was the beginning of the First Great Evangelical Awakening.

John Wesley traveled an estimated 250,000 miles on horseback in every kind of British weather to preach 40,000 messages. He wrote 233 books. Charles Wesley composed 9,000 hymns. George Whitefield in many ways out did even John Wesley. By general acclaim, he was by far the better preacher. Thousands came to faith through his preaching. By the grace of God and the power of the Holy Spirit, all three were indefatigable! In this Great Awakening, there were a great number of leaders inspired by the Holy Spirit. These three were a kind of first fruits.

We should note the extraordinary link between the Reformation with Martin Luther, and the Moravian revival with Count Zinzendorf, and the First Great Evangelical Awakening with the Wesley's and Whitefield. The link is explained by the Builder of the Church, the Messiah Jesus, who has launched every one of these divine initiatives.

### A Burden Has to be Conceived By the Holy Spirit

Is it fanciful of me to write to those who are living in the United States, that if once the Lord were to bring you into *real* intercession, it will not have to do with America continuing to be a superpower? It is not just "God bless America." It is in fact deeply related to the coming of the Lord. It is the fulfillment of the purpose of God not only for the United States, but for the nations and, of course, above all for the Church and for Israel.

I do not know if what I have written resonates in you. Are you an intercessor? Do you want to be an intercessor? If you are going to be an intercessor, it is not just a little time once a day, once a week or once a month; it will cost you your life. For you to conceive the burden that is in the heart of *the* Intercessor by the Holy Spirit is no small matter. Once it is conceived in you by the Holy Spirit, you cannot get rid of it! It remains like a huge pain within your spirit and the only way you can get relief is by interceding, by the pouring out of your heart. In this manner, you will obtain relief, until the burden is back again. Such is an intercessor.

### Take The First Personal Step

Let me say again, we as the church have failed miserably. We have been so comfortable and so happy with our Christianity. The fact is that Jesus is very often outside, knocking on the door. How long shall we go on like this, or shall we do something about it? Only the Lord can fill us with His Spirit and with an understanding of what His will is. We are moving into a world that will be a very different world, and I am not sure we can turn back the time. It is however possible for great awakenings and for revivals to take place in nations like the States, or the United Kingdom, or the Netherlands, or Germany, or the Scandinavian countries. Some of these nations have seen tremendous triumphs of the gospel and nationwide awakenings in their past. Today, however, where are the intercessors?

There is an old Chinese saying: "A journey of a thousand miles begins with one step." The step that we need to take is personal, not corporate. We have to say to the Lord, "Lord, I want to be an intercessor." The Lord is so short of candidates that He will snap you up instantly! There are not too many people who want to be candidates for intercession. However once you say it, He will take you. I thank God that I began very early. I had not been saved very long when I joined a Nepal prayer meeting at fourteen years of age. They were all dear old white-haired people. The other young people said to me: "You are not going to spend one evening a week with those old fogies, are you?" I replied, "Yes." To which they answered: "You must be nuts!" So I said, "We are praying about Nepal, that it will be opened to the gospel." They said, "It will never open, not in a thousand years. It is a Hindu country, and the Royal Family is Hindu, and it will never change."

Nevertheless, I continued going week after week. We prayed for Dr. O'Hanlon and Lucy Steele who were waiting on the slopes of the mountains that divide Nepal from India. They believed the Lord had told them that there would come a day when they would enter Nepal. I shall never forget when the cable came from them: "Tomorrow we go over into Nepal and we are being allowed to set up a clinic there." It was the beginning of a whole work of God. At that point I was fifteen to sixteen years of age and you cannot believe how proud I was. I told all those young people: "You see, I was part of a prayer meeting that saw a closed country opening to the gospel."

It does not matter how young you are. It is best to start when you are young because truthfully if you are going to be real prayer warriors and intercessors, you need to start young. Those of you who are older, do not give up. Maybe you have never been an intercessor, but even you could be a candidate. You would be surprised what the Lord can do with you, once you say: "I am ready." I believe this is the challenge to us in this situation which the western nations are facing. The only answer to this is to discover what the will of God is, and if it is an awakening, to come together in intercession until it happens.

## MAY THE LORD CHALLENGE US

If we are going to see something happen in our nations it is going to cost us. Do not think we can just spend a little time, say a few prayers and then go. It will cost and only the Lord can enable us to endure with patience until He finally does it. However, that He is able to do it, there can be no doubt whatsoever. Let us accept the Lord's challenge and be those who really serve Him in this hour of great need. May the Lord never have to say of this generation: *And I sought for a man among them, that should build up the wall, and stand in the gap before me for the land, that I should not destroy it; but I found none* (Ezekiel 22:30).

# Chapter Six

## THE TWO-FOLD PROMISE OF GOD TO ABRAHAM

And he [Stephen] said, Brethren and fathers, hearken: The God of glory appeared unto our father Abraham, when he was in Mesopotamia, before he dwelt in Haran. (Acts 7:2)

Now the Lord said unto Abram, Get thee out of thy country, and from thy kindred, and from thy father's house, unto the land that I will show thee: and I will make of thee a great nation, and I will bless thee, and make thy name great; and be thou a blessing; and I will bless them that bless thee, and him that curseth thee, will I curse: and in thee shall all the families of the earth be blessed. (Genesis 12:1-3)

For this cause it is of faith, that it may be according to grace; to the end that the promise may be sure to all the seed; not to that only which is of the law, but to that also which is also of the faith of Abraham, who is the father of us all (as it is written, A father of many nations have I made thee) before him whom he believed, even God, who giveth life to the dead, and calleth the things that are not, as though they were. Who in hope believed against hope, to the end that he might become a father of many nations, according to that which had been spoken, So shall thy seed be. (Romans 4:16-18)

The second Psalm is a prophetic window on this Battle of the Ages, and especially on our present situation:

Why do the nations rage, and the peoples meditate a vain thing? The kings of the earth set themselves, and the rulers take counsel together, against the Lord, and against his anointed [His Messiah], saying, Let us break their bonds asunder, and cast away their cords from us. He that sitteth in the heavens will laugh: The Lord will have them in derision. Then will he speak unto them in his wrath, and vex them in his sore displeasure: Yet I have set my king upon my holy hill of Zion. I will tell of the decree: the Lord said unto me, Thou art my Son; This day have I begotten Thee. Ask of me, and I will give thee the nations for thine inheritance, and the uttermost parts of the earth for Thy possession. Thou shalt break them with a rod of iron; Thou shalt dash them in pieces like a potter's vessel. (Psalms 2:1-9)

May we have a word of prayer:

*Beloved Lord, we want to thank You that we are here in Your presence and when You are present anything can happen. We commit ourselves to You for this time. We believe You have something on Your heart that You want to speak to us, to share with us. Our prayer, Lord, is that the anointing which You have so dearly won for us at Calvary may be ours in full portion both for the speaking of Your Word and for the hearing of it.*

*Lord, touch our hearts this evening. We have been talking about intercession and we pray that in some way You will bring us to an understanding of what Your purpose is for Israel and how we can intercede for that people and that land. And we ask all this in the name of our Lord Jesus. Amen.*

### THE BATTLE OF THE AGES

I have entitled this book *The Battle of The Ages* for a reason. It does not matter where you turn in world history, it is part of this battle. It began before the fall of Adam and Eve with a rebellion of a third of the Angels inspired and led by Satan. With mankind's fall beginning with Adam and Eve, the battle became centered on this planet we call Earth. It is a battle between the Living God and Satan, between Light and Darkness, between Good and Evil, between the Truth and the Lie. It is the story of the war between the Redeemed of God, the followers of the Lamb, and those who support and follow Satan. From Genesis chapter one to Revelation chapter twenty two, we have the record of this enduring war. Everyone saved by the grace of God has been catapulted into this vast and ongoing battle, whether we are aware of it or not! In that salvation the Lord has provided us with the covering which is necessary for our safety and the weapons which are necessary for our victory. He has not left us as orphans in this cruel and savage war, but has said that the Father and the Son by the Holy Spirit will dwell in us, enabling us to overcome (see John 14:16-20, 23; 16:33).

The last book of the Bible, the Apocalypse or Revelation, focuses on the climax of the battle of the Ages. It begins with the incredible vision of the Lamb of God "as it had been slain," the Lion of the tribe of Judah forever enthroned. He has already won the battle! From that position of absolute triumph, we see the fury of Satan unleashed upon the nations, and particularly upon the Church and Israel. It is Satan's last attempt to dethrone the Lord Jesus and to win. It ends with the absolute triumph of the Almighty. The City of God, the New Jerusalem, descends from heaven having the glory of God. That City is adorned as a bride for her husband. The Lord has finally and forever won the battle. It is the beginning of a new heaven and a new earth wherein dwells righteousness. All that belongs to the former Ages, the long parenthesis of sin, darkness, and evil, has come to an end.

> Death shall be no more; neither shall there be mourning, nor crying, nor pain anymore: the first things are passed away. And He that sitteth on the throne said, 'Behold, I make all things new' (Revelation 21:4-5)

## A BIRD'S EYE VIEW OF
## GOD'S PURPOSE FOR ISRAEL AND THE NATIONS

I have no doubt that most of you who have read this book so far, know that the whole question of Israel is a point of fierce controversy amongst Christians. Many Christians believe that there is absolutely no future for the Jewish people. They believe that when the Jewish people rejected Jesus as the

Messiah, God rejected them. For them the survival of the Jewish people in history is a sad and abject reminder of what happens to those who reject the purpose and will of God. They are forever forsaken, hated, despised, and given up by God to continuous trouble and affliction.

Those who hold this view consider the recreated State of Israel on the present world scene as not a fulfillment of God's prophetic word, but a colossal mistake and the cause of untold conflict, war, and trouble in the Middle East in particular and in the world in general. In a word, there is no Divine future for the Jewish people. The whole purpose of God is centered in the Church alone, and all the prophetic Scriptures in the Old Testament which speak of Israel's future regathering are to be spiritualized as for the Church.

In this chapter, I want to present a bird's eye view of the whole purpose of God for both Israel and the nations. How is that purpose for both Israel and the Gentiles interlocked? In order to come to a full understanding of God's aim and intention in this matter, it requires both a recognition of God's purpose for the Jewish people, and a recognition of the ingathering of the Gentiles into that same purpose. The determination of God from the beginning was to produce a New Man, saved by the grace of God and indwelt by the Lord Jesus through the Holy Spirit. In that New Man **in Christ**, there is neither Jew nor Gentile, but Christ is everything in everyone! (see Ephesians 2:13-19 cp. Colossians 3:10-11). The birth and life of the Messiah, His death, resurrection, ascension, and enthronement at the Father's right hand was and is pivotal to the fulfillment of this plan. The pouring out of the Holy Spirit by the glorified Messiah fifty days after His death (Pentecost) was the guarantee of the success of this plan!

# The Two-Fold Promise of God to Abraham

## A GREAT TURNING POINT IN DIVINE HISTORY

When the God of glory appeared to our father Abraham while he was in Ur of the Chaldees in Mesopotamia, one of the most extraordinary events in the whole history of mankind took place (Acts 7:2). According to one Jewish tradition, Abraham's family had a lucrative business as idol makers in Ur of the Chaldees. There were idols for everything and for every place; they were on every street corner of Ur, which was no mean city. They were in the temples, in gardens, in homes, in the bedroom, and in the kitchen. There were few places in which there was no idol. If this tradition is true, the business of Abraham's family was an incredibly lucrative business!

According to that story, Abraham was a super salesman in the family business. At some point the God of glory appeared to him (Acts 7:2). It was the Everlasting and Living God, who has neither beginning nor end, who met Abraham. When the Lord met Abraham, he never touched another idol for the rest of his life. We know that when the God of Glory appeared to him, Abraham foresaw in Him the redemption and salvation of the world; he foresaw the day of the Messiah Jesus! For the first time Abraham understood that God had a purpose for mankind and that purpose was going to be fulfilled through the Messiah. Furthermore in the God of Glory, Abraham saw the City of glory. The Hebrew letter tells us that, *he sought for the city which has **the** foundations* (in Greek *the* is accented) *whose builder and architect is God* (Hebrews 11:10).

The moment God appeared to Abraham, it changed his whole life and it changed the whole world. From that point Abraham became a pilgrim, seeking that City of God. Something had happened to him which had spoilt him for anything less than God's highest and best. From being an inhabitant of a great worldly city, an entrepreneur within it seeking wealth and fame, he became a shepherd and a

97

goatherd, a herder of camels. When the God of Glory met him, Abraham was spoilt for anything less than God's eternal purpose. It was as if he was born again. His testimony is like the testimony of the apostle Paul two millennia ahead of him; he considered everything past as loss for the excellency of the knowledge of the Lord.

Many Christians relegate Abraham to history and to the Jewish people; but in actual fact what happened was astounding when you begin to realize it. This was one of the greatest turning points in divine history. Up to that point God had dealt with individuals, with families, and with clans, but He had not dealt with a people. However the moment God saved Abraham, it was with a people in view—the redeemed of the world, both Jew and Gentile.

One of my close friends Malcolm Hedding, former director of the International Christian Embassy in Jerusalem, in a moment of inspiration, has stated it in this way: "When God saved Abraham, He put within him the whole DNA of world redemption." That is why the apostle Paul, next to the Lord Jesus, the greatest Rabbi who ever lived, actually says that Abraham was saved by faith, not by the law (Romans 4:13). It is because Abraham believed with his whole heart in the God whom he had met. He fully trusted in the word that God gave Him. The Scripture says, *And Abraham believed God, and it was reckoned unto him for righteousness* (Romans 4:3). It is the same living faith through which every true believer has ever come into the salvation of God. *For by Grace have you been saved through faith; and that not of yourselves, it is the gift of God* (Ephesians 2:8). All who have been saved by the grace of God have been justified in the sight of God because of this gift of living faith. In this incredible manner, Abraham has become the father of all who put their trust in the Lord and in His Word. It is important that we should understand that Abraham is not merely a great historical figure, but he is called the **father** of all who believe. There is an intimate connection between Abraham and everyone who has been justified by saving faith, both Jew and Gentile. In this sense, his DNA is in everyone who is saved by faith, and where there is full surrender to the Lord and complete obedience to Him, the same spiritual character is formed.

We know that God had said that in Abraham's seed all the nations of the earth would be blessed (see Genesis 22:18), but at that point he had no seed. He tried to work it out with Sarah's help, which was a great disaster, and it resulted in Ishmael. Thank God the Lord can save the seed of Ishmael and is powerfully doing so. However the fact of the matter is that it was a dreadful mistake until Isaac, the son of divine promise, was born. Then God put Abraham to the test and said to him, "Now sacrifice your son, the son of promise" (see Genesis 22:2). Abraham knew very well that the whole promise of God concerning world redemption was centered in his son Isaac. For him to put that son to death would have been tantamount to destroying the whole purpose of God. The Hebrew letter tells us that he believed God would work a miracle of resurrection, and that after he had sacrificed his son, the Lord would bring him back to life and restore him in order that His purpose would be fulfilled (Hebrews 11:17-19). In this event we have a remarkable foreshadowing of the resurrection of the Messiah Jesus.

## THE TWO-FOLD PROMISE OF GOD TO ABRAHAM

It is of the upmost importance that we understand that when the God of glory spoke to Abraham it was a twofold promise which He gave to him. He said unto Abraham:

> Get thee out of thy country, and from thy kindred, and from thy father's house, unto the land that I will show thee: and **I will make of thee a great nation**, and I will bless thee, and make thy name great: and be thou a blessing; and I will bless them that bless thee, and him that curseth thee will I curse: and **in thee shall all the families of the earth be blessed** (Genesis 12:1-3, author's emphasis).

The Lord did not merely promise "I will make of thee a great nation," but also promised that "in thee shall all the families of the earth be blessed." The first prophetic promise was concerning Israel, and the second prophetic promise was concerning the Gentile nations worldwide out of whom multitudes would come into the salvation of God through the Messiah of Israel.

When the Lord Jesus spoke to the Samaritan woman at Jacob's well near Shechem, He said, *We worship that which we know; **for salvation is from the Jews*** (John 4:22, author's emphasis). The Messiah was declaring that salvation is Jewish! We must therefore be very careful that what God has made one, we do not divide. From the moment the Lord spoke to Abraham, it is clear that His purpose was not only to do with Israel but also with the calling out of the Gentiles through Israel into the salvation of God. It is clear that it is all to do with **one divine purpose**. From this we clearly understand, that from the beginning in choosing and in forming Israel, God had not only the salvation of Israel in mind, but also the salvation of the Gentiles.

Psalm 2 is a prophetic window upon this battle of the ages. No matter where we look in this Psalm it speaks of God's eternal purpose and the rage of the Satanic forces of darkness against it. Those spiritual powers of evil inspire national leaders, governments, and powerful individuals to come against the Word of God, the Purpose of God, and the Messiah of God. By the spiritual manipulation of human beings, Satan seeks to triumph and extinguish everything which is of God (see Psalm 2:1-3). In spite of this furious battle, the Lord calmly says:

> He that sitteth in the heavens will laugh; the Lord will have them in derision. Then will he speak unto them in his wrath, and vex them in his sore displeasure: yet I have set my king upon my holy hill of Zion. (Psalm 2:4-6)

The enthroned Messiah is the guarantee that the entire purpose and will of God is going to be fulfilled both for the Jewish people and for the nations.

Here in this small Psalm of twelve verses is an incredible revelation. We know from the Word of God, that Israel is called many times "the inheritance of the Lord." She is His inheritance both by divine choice and election, and by salvation. However in the midst of this battle, God reaffirms His purpose to bring a multitude which no man can number out of the Gentile world.

> I will tell of the decree: The Lord said unto me, thou art my son; this day have I begotten thee. Ask of me, and I will give thee the nations for thine inheritance, and the uttermost parts of the earth for thy possession. (Psalm 2:7-8)

We should carefully note that the Hebrew for *nations* is "Goyim," which can also be translated in English as *Gentiles*. To His inheritance Israel, God the Father adds the redeemed out of all the nations. This was from the beginning the purpose of God.

### A GREAT NATION

What did God mean when He said to Abraham, "I will make of you a great nation"? The God of Glory promised Abraham that out of him should come a great nation. What did He mean and wherein lies Israel's greatness? By normal standards Israel could never be described as a great nation.

The Battle of the Ages

Throughout history she has never had the architecture that for example made Egypt, Babylon, Greece, or Rome great. Her population never matched the population of those great empires. In what then is her greatness? Her greatness lies in the fact that through her alone of all the nations, God's salvation and purpose was to be revealed. She was to be the vessel through which the light of God and the salvation of God was to come to all the world. It was in her that the God of Glory touched this fallen earth for the first time (Exodus 40:34-38; Numbers 9:15-23; II Chronicles 5:13-14; 7:1-3), and with her God made eternal covenants. Through Israel, He made the Noahic rainbow covenant with the world (Genesis 9:8-17); He made the everlasting covenant with Abraham over his seed and the Promised Land (see Genesis 15:17-21). He made the Mosaic covenant with the children of Israel and gave to the world the essential Law of God (Exodus 20:1-21); He made the Davidic covenant concerning the Messiah who would reign for eternity (Isaiah 9:6-7). Through Israel, He gave the New and Eternal covenant (Jeremiah 31:31-34). For this reason we are repeatedly reminded in the New Testament that the Gospel is to the Jew first and then to the Greek (or the Gentile). Through Israel the Word of God, the Law of God, the service of God, and the promises of God were given. Supremely, it was through her that the Savior of the world, the Messiah, was to come, and beginning with her the Gospel was to be preached in all the earth. It was God's salvation for the Gentile nations which came through that little nation, and God's whole eternal purpose was revealed in and through her. No other nation on the face of the earth has this greatness. It makes Israel unique and the only nation with such a claim.

## *The Whole Bible, Humanly Speaking, Came Through Jewish Hands*

We have already clearly stated that God chose Israel to be a vessel through which His light should come to the whole world. Nearly every book of the sixty six books and writings of the Bible has come to the world, humanly speaking, through Jewish hands. **It was of course the Holy Spirit who inspired them. He was the real author!** However, it comes as a shock to some believers of Gentile extraction that the Holy Spirit used Jews! They naturally think that the New Testament is far superior, because it was produced by Christian and Gentile hands, whereas the Old Testament was written by Jewish hands. That makes it suspect. "You must be careful of Jewish exaggeration! Jews make things seem better than they really are in order to win a deal." Apparently the New Testament is nothing like that. There you have absolute precision and accuracy! However they altogether forget that it is not just the thirty-nine books of the Old Testament that were written through Jewish hands, but also the twenty-seven books and letters of the New Testament. Matthew, Mark, John, Peter, Paul, James, Jude, and the writer of the Hebrew letter were all Jews. The only possibility of a Gentile hand is Luke, who was a doctor. We are not completely sure about Luke's background. He may have been Jewish or may have long been attached to a synagogue. He may or may not have been circumcised. His gospel and the Acts are the only possibility of a non-Jewish hand. It is incredible that through this little nation God gave us the whole Bible. It is a further evidence of her greatness. The Bible including both the Old and New Testaments, translated into numerous languages and now in the hands of the redeemed all over the world, came to us through little Israel.

## IN THEE SHALL ALL
## THE FAMILIES OF THE EARTH BE BLESSED

When God confronted Abraham, He not only spoke of a Great nation coming out of his seed, but also made a second promise: *In thee shall all the families of the earth be blessed* (Genesis 12:3). In the same manner in which the first promise has been fulfilled and a still greater fulfillment lies in the days ahead, so has the second promise been gloriously fulfilled! From the day of the Jewish Festival Shavuot (Pentecost) when the risen and Glorified Messiah Jesus poured out the Holy Spirit on 120 saved Jews in Jerusalem, the Gospel has been preached throughout the nations. It was not only the Jewish world that was turned upside down but also the Samaritan world. When the apostle Peter preached the Gospel in Caesarea to a whole crowd of Roman officers and soldiers and the Holy Spirit fell upon them and saved them, it was the beginning of the fulfillment of the second promise to Abraham: *In thee shall the families of the earth be blessed* (Genesis 12:3). From Israel it began and went North, South, East, and West. It was born-again Jews filled with the Holy Spirit who took the Gospel to Greece, to Italy, to France, to Germany, and to Britain. According to British Church tradition, Joseph of Arimathea preached the Gospel in Londinium (London), fourteen years after the death and resurrection of the Lord Jesus. Mark took the Gospel to southern India, others to Ethiopia, to Armenia, to North Africa, and elsewhere. From Jerusalem it has gone to the ends of the earth.

The apostle Paul writing by the Holy Spirit to the believers in Rome wrote:

> For I would not, brethren, have you ignorant of this mystery, lest ye be wise in your own conceits, that a hardening in part

hath befallen Israel until the fullness of the Gentiles be come in
and so all Israel shall be saved. (Romans 11:25-26)

It is important to note that the "fullness of the Gentiles" should not be understood as the "times of the Gentiles." The word in Greek *pleroma* refers to the full or complete number of the Gentiles to be saved. "The hardening in part" in some modern translations has been rendered "a partial petrification has taken place in Israel." It seems clear to me that Paul with his enormous insight into the ways of God and the purpose of God in world history, believed that it was God who had hardened and blinded Israel in order to save the Gentiles (see Romans 11:7-10; 30-32). By the Spirit of God, he writes: *As touching the Gospel **they are enemies for your sake**: but as touching the election they are beloved for the fathers* [Patriarchs] *sake, for the gifts and calling of God are irrevocable* (Romans 11:28-29, author's emphasis). The Apostle was stating that a partial petrification of Israel, a hardening in part, would take place so that the divine purpose through them for the salvation of the Gentiles would be fulfilled. It was God's original purpose to use Israel as a means to bring salvation to the whole world. Through their fall and the hardening and blindness that would follow it, making them enemies of the Gospel, the divine purpose would still be fulfilled through them!

So great is the love of God for Israel that He would go to any lengths however severe, to fulfill the original purpose. In the end, multitudes from every human ethnic group will be saved and come into the commonwealth of Israel. The promise to Abraham that "in thee shall all the families of the earth be blessed" is being fulfilled. In the Ephesian letter, the Apostle Paul states:

That ye were at that time separate from Christ [the Messiah] alienated from the commonwealth of Israel, and strangers from the covenants of the promise, having no hope and without God in the world. But now in Christ Jesus [the Messiah Jesus] **ye that once were far off are made nigh in the blood of Christ** [the Messiah]; (Ephesians 2:12-13, author's emphasis).

## Paul then further writes

That the Gentiles are fellow-heirs, and fellow-members of the body, and fellow-partakers of the promise in Christ Jesus [the Messiah] through the gospel. (Ephesians 3:6)

It is astounding when the impact of what the Apostle has prophetically stated dawns on us: "A partial petrification has taken place in Israel until the complete or full number of the Gentiles be come in and so all Israel shall be saved" (author's paraphrase). He infers that until the great evangelistic commission to reach the whole world with the Gospel and to gather in the saved from every ethnic group is completed, God will hold back from the final spiritual salvation of the Jewish people. When that great work of the Holy Spirit is near completion, God will melt the hardening in part, restore full sight, and save the Jewish people. It will also be the glorious work of the Holy Spirit. He will fall on synagogues, upon Yeshivot (Jewish Bible schools), and upon Jews everywhere. This will be an awakening of such unbelievable power and dimension that it will turn Israel upside down and also world Jewry. In that moment when Jewish eyes are opened and they recognize that the Lord Jesus is the Messiah, the key to Jewish history will be placed in their hands. It will firstly result in enormous sorrow, contrition, and repentance, and then enormous joy and jubilation (see Zechariah 12:10-11; Matthew 23:39). The natural olive branches will have been re-engrafted into their own olive tree, into which the wild olive branches (the Gentile believers) have already been grafted (see Romans 11:22-24). Then Israel and the Jewish people will understand the prophetic words of the apostle Paul:

# The Two-Fold Promise of God to Abraham

> I say then, did they stumble that they might fall? God forbid: **but by their fall salvation is come unto the Gentiles**, to provoke them to jealousy. Now if their fall, is the riches of the world, and their loss the riches of the Gentiles; **how much more their fullness**? (Romans 11:11-12, author's emphasis)

We need to note, that if there has been a fall, there is also a coming fullness. The recreation of the State of Israel and the regathering of the Jews from the ends of the earth to that State are but the beginning of that fullness. It is at present a recreation of the State (politically, economically, militarily, and religiously). We await a spiritual recreation.

They will also understand Paul's prophetic statement: *For if the casting away of them is the reconciling of the world, what shall the receiving of them be, but life from the dead?* (Romans 11:15). Carefully note, that if there has been a "casting away" of Israel which has resulted in the reconciling to God and salvation of innumerable Gentiles, there will also be a "receiving of them." That receiving of the Jewish people will be as resurrection life from the dead. It will go through the whole redeemed body of the Lord Jesus in the last phase of world history, however long that may last. Israel will be the last great witness to the inspiration, the authenticity, and the relevance of the Word of God, and the final witness that Jesus is the Messiah, the Son of the Living God.

## A HISTORY OF CONFLICT AND DIVINE PROTECTION

I have entitled this book *The Battle of the Ages*. It is a fact that the moment Israel appeared on the scene of world history she became the focal point of this battle. Satan and the forces of darkness have done everything in their power to destroy this nation. From the beginning, Satan knew that the light of God and the salvation of God were destined to come to the nations through this people and he did everything in his power to destroy them. If he could not annihilate them, he sought to

107

subvert them by making them like the nations around them. The whole history of Israel from its beginnings in the Exodus out of Egypt has been one long story of conflict and war. In the greatest empire of the day, Egypt, Satan had sought to destroy this people by the extermination of all the Jewish male babies and the enslavement of all the Jewish girls. The story never changes, whether it was the Philistines, or the Canaanite tribes, or the great powers like Assyria, or Babylon, or Egypt. Later it was the Hellenic Empire, and then the Roman Empire. The Satanic powers sought by every means to destroy this nation. It seems that the whole hierarchy of evil and darkness was combined to snuff it out by one means or another. The sin or backsliding of Israel always resulted in divine judgments and exiles. It was Satan who subverted Israel through sin and caused the backsliding, and his aim was to force a rift between the Almighty and Israel. In fact, his hope was that the Almighty would finally give up on Israel and desert her.

The most seductive means Satan used was Hellenism, which was humanism in its most beautiful form. It attracted the Jewish people with its beauty of architecture, of the human form, and of the human mind and thought. Through Hellenism Satan nearly succeeded in subverting the whole purpose of God. It was at that point that the Holy Spirit launched a spiritual movement through Simon the Just, one of the great figures of Jewish history. That movement caused a return by the masses of the people to the Word of God, the Purpose of God, and the Law of God. The Hebrew word from which we derive Pharisee means "to be separate." It was a kind of Separatist and Puritan movement. It was a wholehearted return to the Lord Himself and it saved Israel from Hellenism and spiritual extinction! By the time of the New Testament, it had become, as so often is the case with genuinely spiritual movements, a legalistic and outward form of religion, known as the Pharisees. Another similar movement which the Holy Spirit launched to save Israel was the Essenes. They also were a separatist Puritan movement with a great emphasis on purity of heart, mind and body, and above all a return to the Lord and His Word. They had an effect on the New Testament era.

The greatest single movement launched at this point by the Holy Spirit was the Maccabees. All seemed lost and the antitype of the Antichrist, Antiochus IV Epiphanes, was fully in charge of the Eastern Mediterranean and Israel in particular and was following a policy for the total destruction of Judaism. He desecrated the Temple, banned circumcision and the kashrut (kosher) law, and caused a pig to be sacrificed for the daily offering not only in the Temple but in every town throughout Israel. The Holy Spirit fell on the Maccabee family and it resulted in a spiritual revival that swept through the whole of Judaism and finally triumphed. That miracle is remembered every year in Jewish homes in the festival of Hanukkah, the Feast of Dedication. If the Holy Spirit had not used the Maccabees to bring spiritual renewal to Israel, the New Testament story would have been totally different. The forces of darkness and evil had sought so many times to destroy this people but had failed. They had also sought by every means available to destroy the seed which in the end would result in the birth of the Messiah Jesus. It was the grace and mercy of God alone which had protected Israel.

When the greatest exile in Jewish history took place, beginning in the year A.D. 70 and lasting until the twentieth century, the Jewish people not only lost Jerusalem and the Promised Land, but they were scattered to the four corners of the earth. The fury of the Satanic host had not abated, but fell upon the Jewish people wherever they were found. It is a story of massacres, of murder, of discrimination, and of hatred. Anti-Semitism is the world's oldest hatred and is stoked from hell; it is Satan himself energizing human beings. One would have thought that the greatest exile in Jewish history, and all the loss and suffering entailed in it, would have drawn out some compassion and sympathy on the part of the nations. It did not! Instead it resulted in Jews being banned in country after country, and where they were allowed to remain they suffered much discrimination and destruction: the pogroms of Russia and Eastern Europe and the Roman Catholic Inquisition. It is the story of endless suffering. It climaxed finally with the Nazi Holocaust and the industrialized murder of some eight million Jews. The normal figure given is six million, but Simon Wiesenthal himself a survivor of the Holocaust who spent the final years of his life tracking down Nazi murderers, believed that the figure is nearer eight million. In the forefront of the German army were the Einsatz Gruppe who rounded up Jews in villages and hamlets, made them dig deep ditches and then machine gunned them to death, burying them whilst some of them were still alive.

It is a sad and troubling fact, that the Church became one of the main antagonists of the Jewish people and the cause of much anti-Semitism. Both by its teaching and its practice, it stoked the fires that led to so much death and misery. Years ago visiting the great Jewish seminary in New York, I saw a sculpture of an old thorn bush at the entrance. Underneath were written the words in Hebrew: "And the bush burned with fire and the bush was not consumed" (Exodus 3:2). That is the story of this little but great nation. She has survived by the grace and the will of God alone!

# Chapter Seven

## HE WILL SET UP AN ENSIGN FOR THE NATIONS

And it shall come to pass in that day, that the root of Jesse, that standeth for an ensign of the peoples, unto Him shall the nations seek; and His resting-place shall be glorious. And it shall come to pass in that day, that the Lord will set His hand again the second time to recover the remnant of His people that shall remain, from Assyria, and from Egypt, and from Pathros, and from Cush, and from Elam, and from Shinar, and from Hamath, and from the islands of the sea. And He will set up an ensign for the nations, and will assemble the outcasts of Israel, and gather together the dispersed of Judah from the four corners of the earth. (Isaiah 11:10-12)

And He will lift up an ensign to the nations from far, and will hiss for them from the end of the earth; and, behold, they shall come with speed swiftly. (Isaiah 5:26)

Thus saith the Lord Jehovah, [the unmentionable and holy name of the Lord] Behold, I will lift up my hand to the nations, and set up my ensign to the peoples; and they shall bring thy sons in their bosom, and thy daughters shall be carried upon their shoulders. (Isaiah 49:22)

Hear the word of the Lord [the unmentionable name], O ye nations, and declare it in the isles afar off; and say, He that scattered Israel will gather him, and keep him, as a shepherd doth his flock. For the Lord hath ransomed Jacob, and redeemed him from the hand of him that was stronger than he. (Jeremiah 31:10-11)

For I do not desire, brethren, that you should be ignorant of this mystery, lest you should be wise in your own opinion, that blindness in part has happened to Israel until the fullness of the Gentiles has come in. And so all Israel will be saved...Concerning the gospel they are enemies for your sake, but concerning the election they are beloved for the sake of the fathers. For the gifts and the calling of God are irrevocable. (Rom. 11:25-26a; 28-29 NKJV)

## THE MIRACLE HAPPENED

It has been said that when God is going to do something special, He first makes everything difficult, but when He is going to do something extraordinary, He first makes it absolutely impossible! The recreation of the State of Israel on May 14, 1948 (the 5th of Iyar, 5708) and the regathering of the Jewish exiles from the four corners of the earth comes within the category of the absolutely impossible. The rise of the Jewish state came at a point of absolute hopelessness. It was when the Jewish people were at their most brokenhearted, having suffered the loss of at least eight million fellow Jews, that the divine miracle happened! It was not at the climax of great power, or at the point of enormous jubilation, or at the high point of some great success of a Jewish army but at the point of their greatest weakness. It has sometimes been said that it was Jewish bankers who worked the miracle, or the influence of Jewish politicians in various gentile governments, or a number of other explanations which are also given. None of them adequately suffice. It was a divine miracle worked by God Himself. It is recorded that when the Lord turned Jacob into Israel, it was when Jacob was totally incapable and in the grip of the Heavenly Visitor. He could not go back and he could not go forward. He was in a hopeless condition. It was at that point that God worked a miracle, and by his grace turned Jacob into Israel.

There were not so many who survived the Holocaust, but those that did survive were emaciated, brokenhearted, and in so many cases alone, having lost all their loved ones. When they finally returned to their old homes, they were murdered. For example, when the father of Yitzhak Shamir, former Prime Minister of Israel, returned to their family home in Poland, he was murdered by the neighbors. Thus there was no alternative other than Israel!

There were two million little children who had survived
the Holocaust and who had lost their parents and other
relatives and had nowhere to go but Israel. All these survivors
guided by Israeli volunteers found any ship that floated,
however unseaworthy it was, and made the journey back to the
ancient homeland. Between Europe and Israel was the British
navy with orders that by any means they were to stop those
ships arriving in Israel. When those ships were stopped by the
British navy, they were escorted not back to the ancient
homeland but to Cyprus in the Mediterranean, or to Mauritius
off the Southern coast of South Africa. There they were
detained in camps much like the camps they had left in Nazi-
occupied Europe. The fact of the matter is simple, nothing
could stop the flood of Holocaust Survivors reaching Israel
and nothing could withstand the miracle which God had
worked! In the end, Britain in weariness left Israel. When the
British navy finally left Haifa, the Union Jack was flying at
half-mast and inadvertently it was upside down, which is
normally a sign of distress.

## FIVE ARAB ARMIES SEEKING ISRAEL'S DESTRUCTION ROUTED

Almost at the moment that the State of Israel was declared
five Arab armies attacked. They numbered about 81,500
soldiers and three of those armies were trained by the British.
The world held its breath. Great Britain believed that those
five Arab armies were bound to be successful and a terrible
massacre of the Jews in Israel would take place. Those armies
and the nations they came from represented many millions of
Arabs. The Yishuv (the Jewish citizens of the British
Mandated territory) numbered not more than 600,000 of which
6,000 perished in the war. The forces of the Yishuv numbered
35,000 at the height of the war. They had no tanks, no
armored cars, one airplane (a Messerschmitt 109, a one

113

propeller aircraft), and a hand built machine, commonly called the Davidka, which could do little damage but made a colossal noise. It was not only the miracle that had taken place in the recreation of the State of Israel, but the further divine miracle was that the five Arab armies were completely routed by the Israelis. Those armies left so fast that they left many of their tanks, armored cars, and weapons behind. They had also told the Arabs in the Land to move out because they were going to return and destroy the Israelis and the Arab presence would be a hindrance. The Arab refugees to this day have been a colossal problem. Thus by a twofold miracle, Israel was born.

## THE NEVER FAILING GRACE AND MERCY OF GOD

Israel's presence on the world scene has always been miraculous. From the moment God formed her through the seed of Abraham, through Isaac not Ishmael, through Jacob not Esau (see Psalm 105:6-10), the battle began and has never stopped! In all the furious battles that have taken place in her long history, it has been God Himself who has delivered Israel. She could never have been the vessel of the light and salvation of God to the nations, if it had not been for the protecting grace and love of God. Indeed, Israel through her sin and backsliding would have long ago disappeared but for the mercy of God.

The presence of Israel today amongst the nations is a divine sign. There is no other example in world history of a nation which lost its national home, land, and capital city and then after 2,000 years regained them all. Where else in world history can we find a single instance of another nation dispersed into the four corners of the earth and brought back to its original homeland and capital city? Can we attribute that to Jewish economic power, to Jewish manipulation, or to Jewish intelligence? I think it is simpler to believe that it is the hand of the Almighty Himself in world history. In my estimation, there is no other adequate explanation.

Furthermore we have to add to all of this one further fact. In the history of the nations, we find no other people who had lost their mother tongue and after 2,000 years had it miraculously restored. Hebrew had been the religious language of prayer and worship only but not the mother tongue of the people. Today, it is the mother tongue of millions of Israelis. This recreation of Hebrew as the spoken language of a modern nation after its absence for 2,000 years is miraculous. That it was principally the work of one single man, Eliezer Ben-Yehuda, and not a language committee consisting of language experts, only emphasizes the miracle!

## THE BATTLE OVER ISRAEL HAS NOT ENDED

There is one other aspect that is extraordinary about Israel. The battle for her existence, which stretches over the millennia of time, has not ended. The miracle of her recreation in 1948 was accompanied by the War of Independence. It was a miracle that the state was recreated; it was a miracle that the Jewish exiles returned, and it was a miracle that the War of Independence was decisively won by Israel. Since then there have been nine more wars, three of which should have been the destruction of Israel. In every one of those wars Israel has triumphed. If I were to take the whole history of Israel from the time that the Lord spoke to Abraham and said, "A great nation shall come out of thee," until the twenty first century, it would be clear that she has never ceased to be one of the focal points of the battle of the Ages. The presence of Israel on the world scene today is a divine miracle. It is the work of the Everlasting and Living God, and He is saying something loud and clear to the nations of the world!

## AN ENSIGN OR A STANDARD: A TESTIMONY TO GOD'S FAITHFULNESS

The prophet Isaiah clearly prophesies about our time when he says:

> And it shall come to pass in that day, that the Lord will set his hand again the second time to recover the remnant of his people, that shall remain, from Assyria, and from Egypt, and from Pathros, and from Cush, and from Elam, and Shinar, and from Hamath, and from the islands of the sea. And he will set up an ensign for the nations, and will assemble the outcasts of Israel, and gather together the dispersed of Judah from the four corners of the earth. (Isaiah 11:11-12)

Note carefully that the Spirit of the Lord speaks of a **second time** when He brings back the exiled people. The first time was when the Lord brought back the Jewish exiles from Babylon, some thousand miles east of the land of Israel. We are repeatedly told by some Bible teachers that the only prophesied return of the Exiles was the return from Babylon. Isaiah clearly prophesies by the Holy Spirit that there will be a **second return**. This time he mentions, not only the surrounding nations of Israel, namely Iraq, Syria, Egypt, Upper Egypt, Sudan, Libya, Persia and so forth, but also **the islands of the sea** and **the four corners of the earth.** He is speaking of an exile far greater than anything which Israel had experienced until the exile which began in A.D. 70. That exile lasted at least 1,900 years and was truly to the four corners of the earth. There is hardly anywhere in the whole earth where you could not find Jews. The recreation of Israel in 1948 has led to a massive return of Jews not only from neighboring countries but from the ends of the earth. At the declaration of Independence, the population was about 600,000 Jews. Today, in 2014, the population stands at 8,000,000.

Again Isaiah prophesies:

116

## He Will Set up an Ensign for the Nations

> And he will lift up **an ensign** to the nations from far, and will hiss for them from the end of the earth; and behold, they shall come with speed swiftly. (Isaiah 5:26, author's emphasis)

In the previously mentioned prophecy of Isaiah, he had also spoken of an ensign:

> And he will set up **an ensign** for the nations, and will assemble the outcasts of Israel, and gather together the dispersed of Judah. (Isaiah 11:12, author's emphasis)

Isaiah again prophesies and says:

> Thus Saith the Lord Jehovah, behold, I will lift up my hand to the nations, and set up **my ensign** to the peoples; and they shall bring thy sons in their bosom, and thy daughters shall be carried upon their shoulders. (Isaiah 49:22, author's emphasis)

It is of the utmost importance that we understand why the Holy Spirit uses the word *ensign*. The Hebrew word *nes* translated by the English word *ensign,* simply denotes an ensign, standard, or banner. Those who live in a kingdom will understand better what an ensign means. It always flies over the palace of the King or Queen or other royal dwellings when they are in residence. It also flies on the car, on the train, or on the aircraft in which they are traveling. In other words it denotes that the King or the Queen is present!

It is therefore amazing when one realizes that the recreation of Israel after 1,900 years denotes the presence of the King. Of course, He is at present on the right hand of God the Father, but the effect of His presence is seen everywhere. The nation itself may be unsaved and not yet born of God, but the recreation of Israel and the regathering of the outcasts denotes the purpose, the will, and the work of the King. Bringing this people back from the ends of the earth and protecting them in ten wars since its recreation is all the work of the King. To this I must add the recreation of her fertility from desert and wilderness; the extensive re-afforestation of

117

her hills; the restoration of her ecology in large part; the rebuilding of her towns and cities especially Jerusalem; the reinstitution of her Parliament, the Knesset, and of her sovereign and independent government; the establishment of her army, navy and air force, and of her police force and security services. Even the restoration of the former and latter rains beginning in the Mandatory period is the work of the King!

## JEHOVAH-NISSI: THE LORD MY ENSIGN

When Amalek came against the children of Israel, it seemed as if Israel would be totally defeated and destroyed, but Moses said he would go up to the top of the hill with the rod of God in his hand and pray whilst the children of Israel fought with Amalek. It became impossible for him to keep his arms and hands lifted up in prayer during the whole long battle. Aaron and Hur sat Moses on a large stone boulder and standing on either side held up his hands. Thus Israel won the battle. Moses thereafter built an altar on top of the hill and called it "Jehovah-Nissi": the Lord is my banner or ensign (see Exodus 17:15). Once again that banner or ensign denoted that the Lord was present and had worked a miracle. It signaled that the divine purpose for Israel was going to be fulfilled. In the whole of her modern history from 1948 until this day, the ensign of the Lord flies over Israel. There is no other explanation for her existence and triumph. Thus Israel is in herself prophetic. She is the physical and "down to earth" miraculous evidence for the inspiration, the authenticity, and the relevance of the Word of God in the twentieth and twenty-first centuries! The nation may be unsaved but bringing them back from the ends of the earth is in itself a sign of the work of the King. This ensign which the Lord has set up for the nations denotes the simple fact that He is not only at work in the recreation of Israel, the regathering of the exiles, and her

118

ongoing protection, but also that the final and ultimate purpose of the Lord to save her will be fulfilled, however furious the battle.

## THE PROPHET JEREMIAH GOES TO THE HEART OF THE MATTER

The prophet Jeremiah states this truth about Israel very clearly:

> Hear the word of the Lord, O ye nations, and declare it in the isles afar off; and say, He that scattered Israel will gather him, and keep him, as a shepherd doth his flock. For the Lord hath ransomed Jacob, and redeemed him from the hand of him that was stronger than he. (Jeremiah 31:10-11)

Could there be anything more plain and clear than this prophecy? Two thousand five hundred years ago, Jeremiah prophesied that it was the Lord who would scatter Israel and the Lord who would regather Israel and would keep her in the midst of war and conflict. The Holy Spirit is simply stating that it is the Word of the Lord alone which explains the regathering of Israel and her protection. It also means that all who come against Israel, by whatever means, will discover that it is the Word and the Purpose of God against which they are fighting. No matter if it is superpowers, or powerful federations of nations, or individuals, or sadly even Christians, the clear word of God to Abraham will be fulfilled: *I will bless them that bless thee, and him that curseth thee* [Hebrew: devalue, denigrates, or belittles] *will I curse:* [in Hebrew the strongest word for curse]; (Genesis 12:3). The Holy Spirit through Jeremiah underlines the simple and stark fact that it is the Word of God which is the beginning and the end of the history of Israel. Since Abraham, we have four millennia of history. In all that time, the Lord has watched over this nation. He has twice regathered her which simply means that in some mysterious and unfathomable manner Israel is directly related to the entire fulfillment of the purpose of God.

## THE MESSIAH JESUS ENTHRONED IN ZION

I have already mentioned in the previous chapter that Psalm 2 is a prophetic window on the battle of the ages. It is sobering to recognize that Israel is an ensign to the nations, and the king is enthroned in Zion. In the midst of all the rebellion, the conflict and the opposition to the Word and Purpose of God, The Lord says: *Then will he speak unto them in his wrath, and vex them in his sore displeasure: Yet I have set **My king upon My holy hill of Zion*** (Psalm 2:5-6, author's emphasis). The Lord Jesus is enthroned at the right hand of the Father. He was born King of the Jews, He was acclaimed King of the Jews, and when He died the only words placed above His head were: "Jesus of Nazareth, the King of the Jews." Since He arose from the dead and ascended to the right hand of God, He has reigned as King of Kings and as Savior of the world and still reigns as King of the Jews; He has never abdicated (see Isaiah 9:6-7). In the most quoted Psalm in the New Testament, the Father said: *The Lord saith unto my Lord, sit thou at my right hand until I make thine enemies thy footstool. The Lord will send forth **the rod of thy strength out of Zion***: rule thou in the midst of thine enemies (Psalm 110:1-2, author's emphasis). At some point, the enthroned King, the Lord Jesus, will arise from the throne and fulfill the prophecy of the apostle Paul: *And so all Israel shall be saved: even as it is written, there **shall come out of Zion the deliverer**; he shall turn away ungodliness from Jacob* (Romans 11:26, author's emphasis). When the apostle Paul wrote, "Even as it is written," we are usually referred by Bible teachers to Isaiah 59:20: *And **a Redeemer** will come **to Zion**, and **unto them that turn from transgression in Jacob**, saith the Lord* (author's emphasis). The English translation of the original Hebrew is a

120

correct translation. This prophecy was literally fulfilled when the Messiah Jesus, the Redeemer, came to the physical Zion and saved Jews who turned from transgression in Jacob! This was the early Church which was entirely Jewish.

However, the Apostle writes something quite different! He writes: *Even as it is written, there **shall come out of Zion the Deliverer;** he shall turn away ungodliness from Jacob.* I have looked at the Septuagint (LXX), the ancient translation of the Hebrew Old Testament into Greek, but I have never found Paul's rendering. I therefore have come to the conclusion that Paul, who was not only a great Rabbi, Apostle, and teacher but was also a prophet, was actually prophesying. If that is so, then the Holy Spirit is informing us that there is coming a day when the King, who recreated Israel, is going to arise from the throne at the Father's right hand and, as the Deliverer of Israel, will turn away ungodliness from Jacob and save her. In that day, multitudes will be born of the Spirit of God. It will take a spiritual blockbuster of enormous magnitude to bust the bondage of "the hardening in part," "the partial petrification of Israel" and the blindness placed upon them. Pentecost was such a blockbuster. It turned 120 brokenhearted mourning Jews into a force which was to turn the world upside down.

In my estimation, this is going to happen again. There is nothing that can withstand the power and the person of the Holy Spirit. God the Father is the origin of everything; all was through and for the Son, and the Holy Spirit has always been the supervisor of all the practical work of God. The Holy Spirit brought the world we know out of formlessness and chaos into something of incredible beauty and design. He authored the written Word of God and watched over its transmission through the millennia of time. He brought about the birth of the Lord Jesus; He enabled Him to endure the cross and finish the work of our salvation. He also raised Him from the dead. At Pentecost, He supervised the mission which has reached the ends of the earth. When the King arises from his throne in Zion, it will be the Holy Spirit who finally will watch over the last stages in the fulfillment of God's eternal purpose.

### WE ARE VERY NEAR THE END

Although we have not yet seen the complete number of the Gentiles coming into the salvation of God, we are rapidly moving into the last phase of world history as we know it. This unending and vast battle of the ages, which began not long after the creation of this universe, is finally reaching its climax. The last book of the Bible sometimes called the Apocalypse, which means "the unveiling", in Revelation chapter twelve reveals that Satan, called the deceiver of the whole world, was cast down to the earth with his angels and knows that his time is short. In that time, shortened by the grace of God, his wrath and fury will reach new depths of intensity. He knows very well that his time is short! In the midst of this, we hear a great voice in heaven, saying:

> Now is come the salvation, and the power, and the kingdom or our God, and the authority of his Christ: for the accuser of our brethren is cast down, who accuseth them before our God day and night. And they overcame him because of the blood of the Lamb, and because of word of their testimony; and they loved not their life even unto death. (Revelation 12:10-11)

Simply stated, it means that the Almighty has won the battle.

### THE BURDEN OF THE WORD CONCERNING ISRAEL

The Prophet Zechariah wrote of a burden of the word of the Lord concerning Israel, which had been laid on him (see Zechariah 12:1). It is remarkable that some twenty five hundred years ago, God placed a heavy burden on one of His servants concerning the future, the safety, and the salvation of Israel. This word of the Lord through Zechariah is more contemporary and relevant than tomorrow morning's newspaper! In this prophecy, the Lord places his finger on the heart of the problem and crisis for the Middle East, and indeed for the world. The central point of the conflict is Jerusalem: *Behold, I will make Jerusalem a cup of reeling unto all the peoples round about, and upon Judah also shall it be in the siege against Jerusalem* (Zechariah 12:2). By the Spirit of God, Zechariah speaks of a goblet of wine into which a drug or poison has secretly been added. This was a reference to the favorite way of assassinating enemies, adversaries, or those who were obstacles to your policy at the time. For this reason, every emperor or sultan had a cup bearer (or taster) who tasted the wine before they did. If they keeled over, they knew that there was poison in the wine! This way of removing unwanted leaders was very prevalent in the ancient world, and it would have been very difficult for a cup bearer to get an insurance policy! The Holy Spirit uses this graphic picture to warn the powers that be. It is true that every Empire, Superpower, nation, or people who have meddled with the divinely appointed destiny of Jerusalem have discovered that they have committed suicide or rendered themselves insensible! It is certainly true of all the nations around Israel and the much larger powers who by their plans, strategies, and ideas have been seeking to interfere with God's will and purpose. Even the division of the Promised Land, as well as the division of Jerusalem, comes into this category. They think they are drinking a fine wine, but they will discover that God Himself has mixed a poison with it. They are unwittingly bringing a divine judgment and destruction upon themselves.

## THE SIEGE AGAINST JERUSALEM AND JUDAH

Zechariah prophesies about a "siege against Jerusalem and Judah." Whether this siege means war, conflict, and armies coming against Jerusalem or means the Palestinian National Committee's global plan to strangle Israel economically by boycotts, divestments, or sanctions, the aim is the same: to isolate, destroy, and finally eliminate Israel. This surrounding of Israel by forces that want to destroy her by one means or another, is a real factor in the present situation. Are we seeing the beginning of this siege? Zechariah also prophesies:

> And it shall come to pass in that day, that I will make Jerusalem a burdensome stone for all the peoples; all that burden themselves with it shall be sore wounded; and all the nations of the earth shall be gathered together against it. (Zechariah 12:3)

It is absolutely clear that the recreated Israel is a burdensome stone for all the peoples. Witness the problems in the United Nations expressed in the resolutions concerning Israel and especially Jerusalem. This is only the beginning of a movement to force Israel to comply with the wishes of the nations.

Through Zechariah, the Lord prophesies that any superpower, federation of nations, such as the United Nations or the European Union, or any single nation or people, who meddle with the divine destiny of Jerusalem, will discover they have ruptured themselves. Seeking to remove her from her divinely given position to another position more "acceptable" to them, they will ensure themselves that they will never lift again! It happened with the Ottoman Empire, with the British Empire, and with the Soviet Union. At present, the United States, the European Union, and the United Kingdom are in danger of the same result.

## THE LORD WILL NOT DESERT ISRAEL

A careful reading of Zechariah's prophecy in Zechariah chapter twelve reveals that the Lord does not desert Israel. Instead, He speaks of miraculous deliverances. Far from being destroyed or annihilated, Israel triumphs over it all by the grace and mercy of God alone. The powers and forces that come against her are destroyed. The English translation of the Latin Vulgate of Zechariah 12:6b puts it so simply: *After all is over, Jerusalem will stand where Jerusalem ever stood.* Zechariah promises miracle after miracle when all seems lost for Israel. He prophesies about all the nations coming against Israel, of the siege of Jerusalem, and of conflict and war. Then He introduces these miracles by three utterly simple words: "in that day" (see Zechariah 12:3-4, 6, 8-9). He promises that the "chieftains of Judah" will lead Jerusalem and Israel to triumph (see Zechariah 12:5-6). The English word "chieftains" is the Hebrew word "*aluf,*" the Modern Hebrew word for Generals. We have here the most remarkable divine promises for those who are in charge of the army, air force, and navy. They will be given unbelievable courage to lead the forces with wisdom, shrewdness, and ability.

## ISRAEL SPIRITUALLY SAVED AND BORN OF GOD

These triumphs and victories are only the introduction to something far greater! Zechariah prophesies:

> And it shall come to pass in that day, that I will seek to destroy all the nations that come against Jerusalem. And I will pour upon the house of David, and upon the inhabitants of Jerusalem, the spirit of grace and of supplication; and they shall look unto me whom they have pierced; and they shall mourn for him, as one mourneth for his only son, and shall be in bitterness for him, as one that is in bitterness for his first-born. (Zechariah 12:9-10)

125

The Battle of the Ages

By the Spirit of God, Zechariah prophesies that in the midst of all this war, conflict, and trouble Israel will be led into the salvation of God. The greatest miracle of all will take place. The apostle Paul states this simply: "And so all Israel shall be saved" (Romans 11:26a). Behind that simple statement lies not only several millennia of battle and suffering but the amazing persistence of the love of God. He has used this nation to bring light to the nations, to bring the Word of God to the whole world, and above all through this nation has brought the Savior of the world to them. Now it is not only vast and innumerable multitudes of Gentiles who have come into the salvation of God. The circle of redemption, which began with Abraham's salvation and produced the nation of Israel and through them has come to the whole world, is completed with the salvation of the Jewish people. The Almighty has won the long battle and fulfilled His purpose.

In my estimation, the simple statement of the apostle Paul: "And so all Israel shall be saved" (Romans 11:26a), includes all, both Jew and Gentile who by the saving grace of God, through the gift of living faith, are in the Good Olive Tree. It is not only the natural branches re-engrafted into "their own olive tree" (see Romans 11:17-24) but also the wild olive branches who have been grafted into that same olive tree.

# Epilogue

## THE MYSTERY OF ISRAEL

> For I would not, brethren, have you ignorant of this mystery, lest ye be wise in your own conceits, that a hardening in part hath befallen Israel, until the fullness of the Gentiles be come in; and so all Israel shall be saved. (Rom. 11:25-26)

> Concerning the gospel they are enemies for your sake, but concerning the election they are beloved for the sake of the fathers. For the gifts and the calling of God are irrevocable. (Rom.11:28-29 NKJV)

### THE MYSTERY OF ISRAEL

The apostle Paul, in writing the Roman letter and explaining the problem which an unsaved Israel presented to many Gentile believers, used the term "mystery" when referring to Israel. Most of those in the church at Rome were Gentiles, saved and born of the Spirit of God, and Paul had a great burden for them that they should not be ignorant of this "mystery"

> For I would not, brethren, have you ignorant of this mystery, lest ye be wise in your own conceits, that a hardening in part hath befallen Israel, until the fullness of the Gentiles be come in; and so all Israel shall be saved. (Romans 11:25-26)

In our understanding of God's full purpose for Israel and His strategy concerning her, we should carefully note the Apostle's use of this word. In Greek it is "mystērion," which with the Latin "mysterium" has come into the English language as "mystery." A mystery is something secret, hidden, and altogether beyond human reason. It has to be divinely revealed. He describes the whole question of Israel as a mystery, necessitating the need of the Holy Spirit's revelation, if we are to understand its spiritual significance. His burden for the church in Rome is that the Holy Spirit would dispel any ignorance that they might have concerning this matter. This is certainly also true for Christian believers and for the Church in the twenty first century and we should heed Paul's burden for dispelling the kind of ignorance that leads to misconception, pride, and a false understanding which in turn leads to a false theology.

The letter to the Romans is the greatest exposition of the Gospel in the sixty-six books and writings of the Bible. It is often stated that the question of the recreated state of Israel as a prophetic fulfillment and a divine act in the twentieth century is not alluded to in the New Testament. Yet Paul, in this remarkable exposition of the Gospel, devotes three whole chapters of the Roman letter out of its sixteen chapters to the question of Israel. At the end of those three chapters, he describes what he has written as: "this mystery" (see Romans 11:25). How does God elect a people and un-elect them; choose them and un-choose them? The Apostle effectively deals with the whole "problem" of Israel. He squarely faces their rejection of the Messiah, the hardening in part that has befallen Israel, the partial petrification that has taken place, and the blindness. Then in these three chapters, he boldly asserts that God has **not** finished with Israel, but speaks of their coming fullness, of their being received again, and of their being re-engrafted into their own olive tree (see Romans 11:12,15, 24). He concludes this matter with these words: *As touching the gospel **they are enemies for your sake**: but as **touching the election** they are beloved for the fathers' sake. **For the gifts and the calling of God are irrevocable** (Romans 11:28-29, author's emphasis). Paul then sums up these three

chapters with the words: *I would not have you ignorant of **this
mystery**"* (Romans 11:25, author's emphasis).

There can be no doubt about Israel being a divine
mystery! The purpose of the Almighty in producing her
through the seed of Abraham, guarding her survival through
the millennia of time in spite of her waywardness, backsliding,
and at times apostasy, is truly a mystery. Her reappearance on
the world scene at the point of her greatest weakness and
desolation, after the greatest exile of her history, makes the
mystery even deeper. What is it about this nation that arouses
the rage and fury of Satan and the forces of evil and darkness?
The controversy, the anger, and the violent opposition over her
reappearance on the world stage and the many attempts to
destroy her which have followed, only make this mystery
more impenetrable. How can God be using an unsaved nation
as a testimony to His faithfulness and power? How can such a
nation be a physical evidence of the total validity of God's
Word, when they have rejected the Messiah? How can He give
her victory in the many times she has faced overwhelming
forces, bent on her total destruction? To the natural mind, it
just does not make sense. Yet this deeply mysterious purpose
proceeding from the Heart and the Mind of God will in the
end be fulfilled.

The apostle Paul with his insight into the ways of God,
believes that the hardening and the blindness in part which has
befallen Israel, is a divine strategy to save the Gentiles. When
that strategy nears its completion, the Lord will remove the
hardening and the blindness with glorious result, and thus all
Israel will be saved. If this is the truth, then the fury over
Israel is explained! It matters not what the Enemy will seek to
do, the Lord Himself will watch over the fulfillment of His
own purpose. In exactly the same manner in which the Holy

Spirit needed to reveal this mystery to the believers in Rome, the Holy Spirit needs to reveal it to us as well.

## PAUL EXPLAINS THE MYSTERY

Incredibly Paul seeks to explain the mystery:

> By their fall **salvation has come to the Gentiles**... Their fall is **the riches of the world** and their loss **the riches of the Gentiles**... The casting away of them is the **reconciling of the world**... Until **the complete number of the Gentiles** be come in. (Romans 11:11-12, 15, 25, author's emphasis)

It is clear that the Apostle is explaining a divine strategy.

Is it any wonder that Paul ends this revelation with this paean of praise and worship:

> O the depth of the riches both of wisdom and the knowledge of God! How unsearchable are his judgements, and his ways past tracing out! For who hath known the mind of the Lord? Or who hath been His counsellor? Or who hath first given to Him, and it shall be recompensed unto Him again? For of Him, and through Him, and unto Him are all things. To Him be the glory forever. Amen. (Romans 11:33-36)

This whole question of Israel, especially its modern reappearance on the world scene is a profound mystery, and we need it to be revealed to us by the Holy Spirit. Then it becomes a cause for worship, praise, and a physical evidence to us of the absolute faithfulness of God.

## About Lance Lambert

Lance Lambert is one of the most distinguished Bible scholars and speakers in Israel today and has an itinerant teaching ministry worldwide.

Born in 1931, Lance grew up in Richmond, Surrey and came to know the Lord at twelve years of age. He entered the school of African and Oriental studies at London University to prepare for work in China. He studied Classical Chinese, Mandarin, Oriental Philosophy and Far Eastern History, but the revolution closed the door to European missionaries and his entry into China.

In the early 1950's Lance served in the Royal Air Force in Egypt and later founded Halford House Christian Fellowship in Richmond, England.

Having discovered his Jewish ancestry Lance became an Israeli citizen in 1980 and now has his home next to the Old City of Jerusalem. His father and many members of his family died in the Holocaust.

Lance is noted for his eschatological views, which place him in the tradition of Watchman Nee and T. Austin-Sparks. He produces a widely appreciated quarterly audio recording called the Middle East Update, which gives his unique perspective on current events in the Middle East, in the light of God's Word. He has written numerous books and is presenter of the video production, Jerusalem, the Covenant City.

FOR OTHER BOOKS AND MESSAGES,
PLEASE VISIT:

www.LanceLambert.org

www.christiantestimonyministry.com

www.Amazon.com (and Amazon worldwide)

www.Barnesandnobel.com

CPSIA information can be obtained at www.ICGtesting.com
Printed in the USA
LVOW10s1802060915

453036LV00027B/1536/P